ANDREAS PALLADIVS VICENTINVS.

Manfred Wundram · Thomas Pape
Photographs: Paolo Marton

ANDREA
PALLADIO

1508–1580

Architect between the Renaissance and Baroque

TASCHEN

HONG KONG KÖLN LONDON LOS ANGELES MADRID PARIS TOKYO

The groundplans are in the "Quattro Libri" by Andrea Palladio
and in the "Fabbriche" by Ottavio Bertotti Scamozzi.

To stay informed about upcoming TASCHEN titles, please request our magazine
at www.taschen.com/magazine or write to TASCHEN America, 6671 Sunset Boulevard,
Suite 1508, USA–Los Angeles, CA 90028, contact-us@taschen.com, Fax: +1-323-463 4442.
We will be happy to send you a free copy of our magazine which is filled with information
about all of our books.

© 2008 TASCHEN GmbH
Hohenzollernring 53, D–50672 Köln
www.taschen.com

Original edition: © 1989 Benedikt Taschen Verlag GmbH
Cover design: SenseNet/Andy Disl and Birgit Reber, Cologne
Maps and plans: Held & Rieger, Fellbach
Photos pages 12/13, 120/121, 124/125: AKG, Berlin

Printed in China
ISBN 978–3–8365–0547–5

Contents

Andrea Palladio
Architect between the Renaissance and Baroque
6

Palladio

Architect between the Renaissance and Baroque

No other architect in western art history has had so spontaneous, and at the same time, through the centuries, so undiminished and enduring an effect as Andrea Palladio. Palladianism crosses every architectural border, not only in Latin countries, but also in Germany, the Netherlands, Scandinavia and Eastern European countries, and forms one of the most important roots of 17th and 18th century English architecture. And although Palladio, throughout his entire creative life, concentrated on "pure" architecture, the forms he defined had an effect on other areas, such as English furniture making of the 19th century.

Such extensive imitation, which over many epochs allowed the work of a single artist to become a distinct style, presupposes that norms were created and models developed that could be passed on independently from his work as an individual. In this respect Palladio is seen as the first "classicist" of modern architecture, as the master, who in his intensive examination of ancient architecture not only sought to revive it for his time, but positively to imitate it and give it a timeless validity.

Palladio himself contributed to a large degree to this assessment and restriction of the view of his work. He not only published in 1554, as a result of his first journeys to Rome, the book *L'Antichità di Roma*, a kind of inventory of the monuments which in the middle of the sixteenth century had been preserved or already rediscovered in Rome, but also admitted in the introduction to his *Quattro Libri dell'Architettura*, which were published in 1570, that he had chosen Vitruvius to be his guide and master, as "in their buildings too, the ancient Romans surpassed all who came after them".

The context in which his buildings are to be seen and understood has to be taken in a considerably broader sense. This was recognised by Goethe amongst others, who on 30th December 1795 wrote to his friend and adviser Heinrich Meyer: "The more one studies Palladio, the more incomprehensible the genius, the mastery, the *richness*, the *versatility* and the grace of this man become." In 1980, on the occasion of the 400th anniversary of the death of Palladio, a series of other catchwords were coined for his work, alongside the labelling of this architect simply as a classicist: Palladio the master, who, under the

"The Doric order of columns started and got its name from the Greek people of the Dorians, who lived in Asia . . . Among the ancients, this order has no pedestals, but does among modern architects . . . This order does not have its own base, which is why it is erected without bases in many buildings, such as the Theatre of Marcellus in Rome, in the Templum pietatis close to that theatre, in the Theatre of Vicenza and in many other places. But the Attic base is occasionally used, which makes it look very much more beautiful . . ."
(Andrea Palladio, 1570, On the Doric order)

influence of northern Italian humanistic circles, sought to realize the ideal of a new Arcadia; Palladio, who as a loyal servant of his feudal clients was able, in his villas and palace façades, to transform general rules of form into an idea; and finally Palladio, in the more strict sense of the history of the style, as a master who, despite his "classicism", was a typical representative of what is known as Mannerism.

All these classifications certainly contain a degree of truth, but like all generalisations do not reach to the centre of his work. Rather, the question that we ask repeatedly should be: of what do Goethe's terms "richness" and "versatility" consist? And moreover: because the architecture of Ancient Rome is doubtless one of the bases of Palladio's work, *what* actually has Palladio taken over from antiquity, and *how* has he related these stimuli, which in each case corresponded to the task and his stage of development of the moment, to his own artistic ideas?

Palladio, whose proper name was Andrea di Piero, was born on 8th November 1508, the son of a Paduan miller. When he was thirteen, his father took out a six-year apprenticeship for him with the workshop of the architect and stonemason Bartolomeo Cavazza da Sossano in Padua. Further details about his education have remained unclear to the present day. In April 1523 Andrea fled from Cavazza's workshop to Vicenza, but was forced to return due to his breach of contract. A year later, the young stonemason was able to join the guild of bricklayers and stonemasons in Vicenza and was admitted to the respected workshop of Giovanni di Giacomo da Porlezza in Pedemuro. At first nothing pointed to a career beyond that of an artisan. The attempt he made in 1530 to start up his own workshop evidently came to grief after a short time. In 1534 Andrea was still a member of the Pedemuro workshop. So on the one hand his remark that he devoted himself to the study of architecture from his earliest years shows his memory to have been influenced by his later success, but on the other hand his long activity as a stonemason ought to have sharpened his feeling for fine shaping and development of detail.

The date of his first meeting in Vicenza with Count Giangiorgio Trissino (1478–1550), who was highly regarded in humanist circles and very active as a writer, is given as 19th February 1538. We know nothing of the personal relations between the young stonemason, who on 26th August 1540 was awarded the title of architect, and the Vicenzan nobleman.

Certainly Trissino must have both gained access for Andrea di Piero to the polite society of Vicenzan clients and have made an extensive study of contemporary and Roman architecture possible for him. In the summer of 1541, he presumably made his first journey with his patron to Rome, which the two of them followed up with a second and lengthier stay from late autumn in 1545 to the early months of 1546. And it was also Trissino who in 1545 gave the architect the name "Palladio", after Pallas Athene, the patron goddess of the arts. During a further stay in Rome from 1546 to 1547, Palladio also devoted himself to studies in Tivoli, Palestrina and Albano. His hopes of gaining a position in the society of masons of St. Peter's in Rome in 1549 fell through with the death of Pope Paul III. In 1554 Palladio presented his work *L'Antichità di Roma* as the fruits of his journeys to Rome.

Palladio's first verifiable activities as an architect began in the 1540s. A series of villas in the vicinity of Vicenza and the major commission for the Palazzo Thiene in Vicenza were followed, on 11th April 1549, by his appointment as the main architect for the so-called basilica, the loggias of the Palazzo della Ragione in Vicenza, which was the first high point of his career. From then on, Palladio was the peer of the older Jacopo Sansovino (1486–1570) and Michele Sanmicheli (1484–1559) as the most important architect in northern Italy, but was soon to outstrip them in his importance in historical development. Palladio's fame spread. His friendship with the Venetian patrician Daniele Barbaro began around 1550, and gained him access to the aristocratic circles of Venice. A journey to Trent in 1552 was prolonged by a stay in Innsbruck on the invitation of the Prince Bishop, Cardinal Christoforo Madruzzi, on whose initiative the Council of Trent took place in 1545.

Anything other than precocious, Palladio reached the height of his career at the beginning of the fifth decade of his life. Thoroughly schooled technically, comprehensively educated in the history of architecture, and with many humanist interests, he was able to develop his fantasy in all directions. There followed in his fifties villas for the Vicenzans, but also for the Venetian aristocracy. The villas of Venetia have to a large degree, albeit by crudely simplifying the facts, become a kind of synonym for Palladio's work. Numerous other architects were active in this area both at the same time and after Palladio.

Above all, however, villa architecture only signified a *new* emphasis in Palladio's work. From the 1560s onwards, palaces and palace façades were added above all in Vicenza, and at the same time Venice, whose "picturesque" basic position in forming palace façades had to remain foreign to Palladio's "classical style", offered him tasks in the field of church architecture: after the cloisters of Santa Maria della Carità were built in 1560–61 and the refectory of the convent of San Giorgio Maggiore in 1560–62, and after the design for the façade of San Francesco della Vigna had been produced after 1562, there followed the laying of the foundation stone for the church of San Giorgio Maggiore in 1565, and start on the work on the pilgrimage church of Il Redentore in 1576 – all of them works whose importance in the development of architecture definitely counterbalances that of buildings of a secular nature.

Palladio's standing amongst his contemporaries rose constantly. In 1556 he had been one of the founding members of the Olympian Academy in Vicenza. In 1566 he travelled as the guest of the Duke Emanuele Filiberto of Savoy to Turin and from there visited Provence. In that same year he was made a member of the Accademia del Disegno in Florence. In 1568 he had to turn down an invitation to the Imperial Court in Vienna due to overwork. In 1570 he became Sansovino's successor as advising architect in Venice.

The wealth of artistic solutions and possibilities of expression

"The Ionic order of columns came into being in the Asian province of Ionia, and it is written, that the Temple of Diana in Ephesus was built with this order . . . As Attic bases were used in many ancient buildings with this column order, which is something that I greatly prefer, I have drawn . . . these Attic bases . . . in over the pedestals . . . At the corners of Ionic colon-

nades or ambulatories, capitals are added, which have volutes not only at the front, but also on those parts which are normally the sides of the capital. These capitals therefore are shaped on two sides. They are called corner capitals. How they are made is something that I shall show in my book about temples . . ."
(Andrea Palladio, 1570, On the Ionic order)

developed more and more in the last two decades of his creative life. Palladio did not create variations on a mastery gained from all sorts of tasks, but advanced from masterpiece to masterpiece into new areas of artistic endeavour. And he constantly took into consideration the requirements made by geographic position and urban development, especially with regard to the visibility of a work and its function. His standing evidently gained him exceptional leeway in dealings with his clients.

In the last year of his life, two of the wishes which had been occupying Palladio's thoughts and designs for a long time were fulfilled: the Olympian Society in Vicenza assigned to him the task of planning a new theatre, the Teatro Olimpico, and his old Venetian friend and patron, Marcanton Barbaro, commissioned him to build a family chapel in the shape of a centralized building near the Villa Barbaro in Maser. Palladio died in the course of this work on 19th August 1580, either in Vicenza or in Maser during his supervision of the work on the Tempietto there.

We know little about Palladio's character — amazingly little for an age in which the lives of artists and anecdotes about them were being recorded ever more frequently. Not even an authentic likeness has come down to us. Matter-of-fact documents inform us about his family life: on 14th April 1534 there is an estimation of the dowry of his wife, who was a carpenter's daughter. The marriage produced four sons — Leonida, Marcantonio, Orazio and Silla — and one daughter, Zenobia. The deaths in quick succession of Leonida and Orazio at the beginning of 1572 evidently affected their father deeply.

Palladio seems to have been friendly, attentive and skilful in his relations both with clients and workers. According to the reports of his contemporaries, he passed on the thoroughness of his education in the Pedemuro workshop to the members of his own workshop, and at the same time was able to give each person a feeling of joy in the task allotted him.

Every attempt to find a key to Palladio's work in his character and life is doomed to failure, just as conversely his works deny us even the smallest hint as to his personality. Palladio therefore from the start escaped the danger of misinterpretation caused by the biographical approach, which has opened up so many false routes to other outstanding artists of the sixteenth century. Palladio the man appears in retrospect to have a similar impersonal status to his works.

Villa Godi

Lonedo di Lugo (Vicenza)

"The following building owned by Signor Girolamo de' Godi is in Lonedo in the region of Vicenza. It lies on a hill with a wonderful view, with a river flowing past which is used by fishermen."

With these words Andrea Palladio introduces his description of the Villa Godi in Lonedo in *The Four Books of Architecture*. This well-preserved building is regarded as one of Palladio's earliest works. Its time of completion, which is assumed to be about 1540, even predates Palladio's first trip to Rome.

Although he had already been prompted to study humanism through his relationship with Giangiorgio Trissino, in this building Palladio shows himself to be rather at odds with the architecture of his time. It is true that the form of the Villa Godi echoes that of his patron Trissino's villa in Cricoli, which Palladio had worked on in his capac-

Below: ground-plan of the Villa Godi from the Quattro Libri. An extensive complex of farm buildings originally belonged to the villa. Of the planned buildings, not much more than the mansion house remains today.

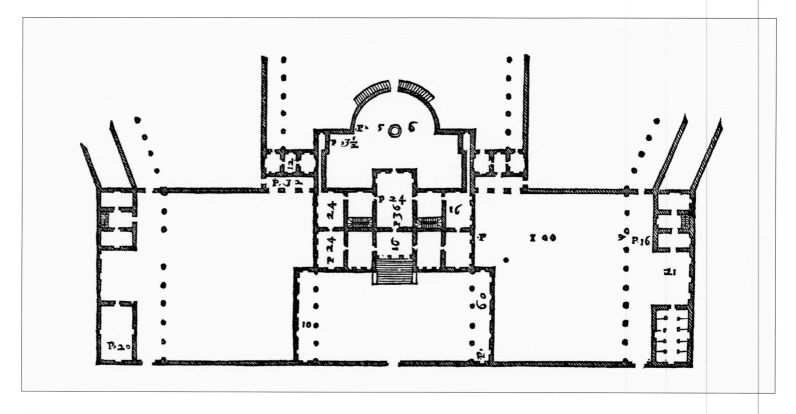

Right: the Villa Godi, seen from the flight of steps of the Villa Piovene: from this perspective the echoing of fortress architecture, which is often found in Venetia, is especially clear.

pp. 12/13: the first work that is certainly of Palladian origin still bears clear characteristics of the architecture of his time. An harmonic unity of landscape and architecture does not yet seem to have been aspired to. The building is a massive block consisting of three separate parts. The representational and living areas are clearly separate from each other and do not present a unified appearance.

Below: view of the façade of the Villa Godi from the Quattro Libri. The actually completed building appears in this sketch in a later modified form. The windows of the risalitos are determined by a regular triple rhythm, the recessed central part rises like a tower above the side compartments.

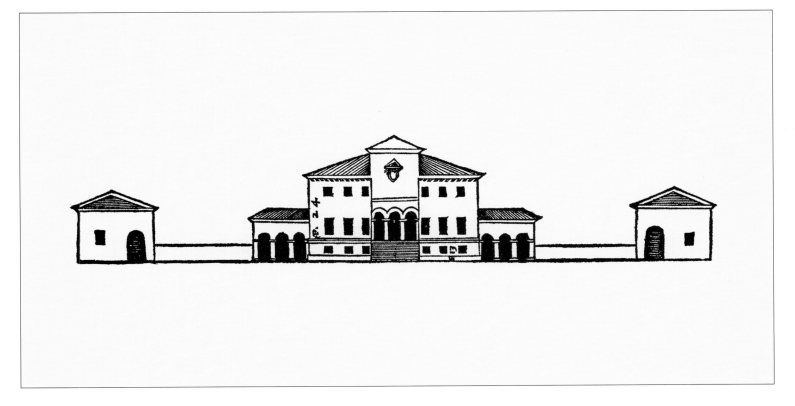

p. 14: view through the triple arcade of the loggia onto the landscape beyond the estate. The Villa Godi is surrounded by a large park. This park was newly laid out in the nineteenth century.

Right: the flight of steps underlines the effect of the risalitos. It is flanked by balusters and in its width corresponds to the middle arcade of the loggia. That this narrow flight of steps allows the recessed central part to completely fade in importance behind the risalitos, is something that Palladio himself seems to have felt in later years: in the Quattro Libri he has a large flight of steps leading up to the loggia.

ity as an architect of the Pedemuro workshop. In both buildings a recessed central part is flanked by two corner risalitos. Also, both buildings are laid out with symmetrical axes. But that it is not a case of one building being dependent upon the other is demonstrated by the totally different way in which Palladio treats the usual type of Venetian two-towered villa: the central part of the villa is pushed like a wedge in between the massive risalitos, each of which is considerably wider than the central part. So the relationship of the risalito and central part, which is represented by the two-towered villa, is reversed.

The overpowering impression of the risalitos is not however based merely upon the actual relationship of the dimensions; the structure of the façade is definitely meant to strengthen this impression. While in Cricoli the symmetrical axis at the same time represents that part of the building to which the modulation of the façade leads one's eyes, in the Villa Godi it marks a parameter of the correspondence in form of those compartments which are ordered to the left and right.

Because of this the risalitos clearly predominate in contrast to the central part of the villa. Even though both the central part and the risalitos are structured by means of a regular rhythm of vertical axes, the groups of double windows on the façades of the risalitos, which

find their counterpart in the windowing forced onto the outer walls of the risalitos, optically counterpoint the central axis of the whole façade. The empty spaces created by the structure of the risalito façades, which distinguish the view of the façade by means of their flat, unworked wall surfaces, cause the risalitos to appear massive to such an extent that it can find no counterpart in the central part of the building. Just the opposite: the piano nobile is broken up by a loggia that is delimited by an arrangement of three arches; in the ground storey two arcade arrangements, which are optically prepared for by blind arches in the lower storey of the risalitos, flank a flight of steps that leads up to the loggia. Two so-called mezzanine or half-storey windows form the conclusion at the top, and the coat of arms of the Godi family is set into the wall between them.

If one walks around the building, one is given just the opposite impression: while the central part is recessed at the front, at the back it projects from the body of the building as a risalito. Palladio must have regarded the body of the building as a clear-cut block, from which nothing could be removed without something else being added at the relevant place. The serliana on this rear façade was not originally intended: it replaced a Roman thermal window in 1550, when Palladio was called in to undertake some alterations in the course of frescoes being added to the sala in the piano nobile.

Above left: framing columns are replaced in the Hall of the Muses by so-called caryatids – monumental figures of women, which function as architectural supports. This painted sham architecture divides the wall into individual painted areas, which are filled with portrayals of muses and poets in Arcadian landscapes. The Hall of the Muses is the only room in the Villa Godi whose fresco decorations were carried out by Battista del Moro.

Above right and p. 17: the ruins of a Greek temple form the backdrop for the depiction of Olympian gods. In the endeavour to revive the ancient world, depictions of gods in Venetian villas were only carried out in such rooms where the greatness and proportion did justice to the dignity of the theme.

pp. 18/19: the "Pax Veneziana" was, after the long period of military conflict, in particular the disorders of the League of Cambrai, both longed for and welcome. This is reflected in many of the fresco cycles in Venetian villas. Scenes were often depicted (as here in the Villa Godi) which symbolized peace and justice.

Villa Piovene

Lonedo di Lugo (Vicenza)

The Villa Piovene was built around 1539—40 in the immediate vicinity of the Villa Godi. It seems reasonable to suppose in it a project in competition with the Villa Godi. And indeed rivalries can be proved to have existed between the Godi and Piovene families, which, perfectly understandable in the terms of 16th century society, were capable of channelling the ambition of Battista Piovene and Tommaso (Battista's son, who probably commissioned the project) into such a course of

Below: the Villa Piovene is not proved by Palladio's architectural treatise to be definitely one of his works, but can in all likelihood be ascribed to him. Its relationship with the Villa Godi is made unclear by the dominance of the loggia. The double-flighted steps, which lead up to the loggia, disturbs the balance of the impression that the façade makes. It is an addition of later years.

action. The Piovene family did, though, seem less intent on comparing the size of their villa with that of the Godi family than in the choice of the workshop carrying out the work, that of Giovanni di Giacomo da Polezza in Pedemuro, who was also responsible for the execution of the work on the Villa Godi.

The Villa Piovene, as can be conjectured from documents, was originally smaller than it appears today: the loggia that projects in the centre – six Ionic columns supporting a triangular gable – was begun by Palladio around 1570 and completed after his death in 1587. The extension of the mansion and the vertical window rhythms can also be assumed to have taken place in the 1570s, and was in accordance with Palladio's wishes, though not carried out by him. The two flights of steps which lead from the lower storey up to the loggia can be attributed to Francesco Muttoni, as can the two farm wings with the "barchesses". Even though Palladio was not accepted as the author without some controversy and should not be assumed to be responsible for the entire estate, the mansion can be regarded as following his plan, which seems to have been carried out in accordance with his wishes at least with regard to the shaping of the façade.

Today the Villa Piovene can be seen against the picturesque backdrop of a garden, which was laid out in the nineteenth century. Situated in the plain of the river Astico, its position was certainly a fortunate choice. The Villa Piovene looks rather simple and unassum-

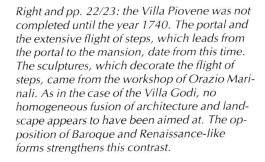

Right and pp. 22/23: the Villa Piovene was not completed until the year 1740. The portal and the extensive flight of steps, which leads from the portal to the mansion, date from this time. The sculptures, which decorate the flight of steps, came from the workshop of Orazio Marinali. As in the case of the Villa Godi, no homogeneous fusion of architecture and landscape appears to have been aimed at. The opposition of Baroque and Renaissance-like forms strengthens this contrast.

ing when seen against the rich lay-out of the garden and the steps, which are decorated with sculptures from the workshop of Orazio Marinali. The impression of disorganized interwoven motifs, which characterizes the front's façade, is confusing. This irritation can indisputably be traced back to later additions to the façade. A Villa Piovene stripped of these later additions shows obvious connections to the Villa Godi, which become all the clearer if one includes the enlargement of the mansion and the outer vertical axes in one's examination. The spacious and shadowy loggia extends over five vertical rhythms and consequently calls forth a visual pressing of the façade structure towards the central axis. Without this loggia both the differences and the similarities of the two neighbouring villas become obvious.

Differing ground-plan lay-outs are countered with a façade structure that is comparable as regards the windows in the stonework. While the central part is recessed in the Villa Godi in order to come out again at the back, the Villa Piovene is built on a rectangular ground-plan. The absence of a risalito causes the outer wings to lose their dominance in favour of the middle part which accentuates the central axis. Nonetheless a large amount of smooth unmodulated wall surface is created on the façade of the Villa Piovene, its calm distinctly ruffled by the later additions, whereas what should be considered as the original façade structure with an arrangement of three arches in the central part of the piano nobile and a simple flight of steps leading up to it would rather have strengthened the impression of order.

Villa Forni-Cerato

Montecchio Precalcino (Vicenza)

The Villa Forni-Cerato is situated in Montecchio Precalcino near Vicenza against a backdrop of fields. The double name which it is always given dates back to 1610. In that year the building belonging to Girolamo Forni, who can be regarded as having commissioned it, passed in accordance with a provision in his will into the ownership of Giuseppe, Girolamo and Baldissera Cerato. Both its attribution to Palladio and the assumption that Girolamo Forni had it built must remain a matter of speculation. It is mentioned for the first time by Francesco Muttoni and Ottavio Bertotti Scamozzi in the eighteenth century that Palladio was the architect who carried out the work. Modern research agrees almost unanimously with these two architects. In addition the villa itself, which was probably built between 1541 and 1542, reveals very clearly who its creator was.

Its present condition testifies to this more impressively than was the case in past centuries. Façade reliefs were removed in 1924, which are recorded by a copperplate engraving by Marco Moro, but do not at all agree with Palladio's formal idiom and can scarcely be considered to

Villa Forni-Cerato: ground-plan and frontal view according to Ottavio Bertotti-Scamozzi. For the first time Palladio presents a clearly defined cube as the core of the building. As can be generally observed in his early works, Palladio arranges the ground-plan in three vertical lines, the middle one being the representational area and the two outer ones indicating the living areas.

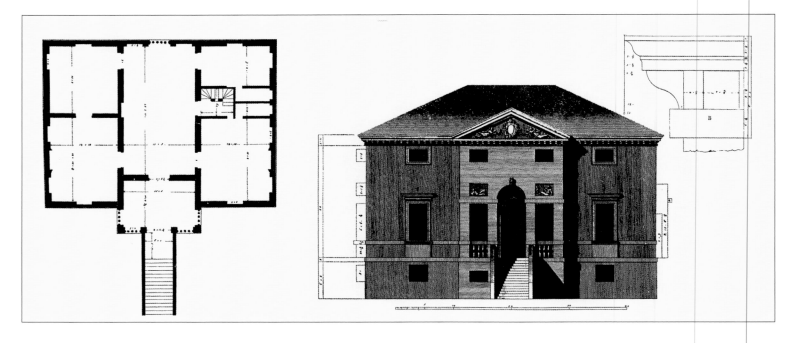

Right: the Villa Forni-Cerato is also one of those buildings which are not identified as Palladio's work in his architectural treatise. He is mentioned as its author for the first time in the eighteenth century. That he should be accepted as the architect who carried out the work is also suggested by stylistic features.

pp. 28/29: the Villa Forni-Cerato can be assumed to have been built around 1541–42. The risalito that protrudes from the core of the building dominates the façade. The two side compartments of the building are harmonically related to it.

have been planned by him. Today only a mask over the round arch of the entrance serliana can be seen of the façade decoration, which can be attributed to Allesandrio Vittoria. The reliefs, which show river gods, are twentieth century copies. The same is true of the coat of arms within the gable area. The body of the building has not undergone any changes with the exception of the back, which had a serliana still visible today, which was to be interpreted as a response to that on the front façade, but was later replaced by a balcony.

The Villa Forni-Cerato is relatively small in size and its height is structured by the triple rhythm of the cellar storey, piano nobile and mezzanine storey. This triple pattern also determines the width of the villa. The loggia stands out as the dominant part of the building on the frontal façade. In what is a remarkable relationship to the Villa Godi, a flight of steps reaches over the basement and leads up to the loggia, which opens in a serliana. This serliana takes up the entire width of the loggia and gives it a special visual importance. The emphasis on the

central axis is exceedingly clear and is not broken by windows forced through the outer walls as in the previous buildings. Just the opposite: the windowing manifestly fits in with the proportional structure of the villa. But it is not only in this respect that the Villa Forni-Cerato marks a considerable step forwards in Palladio's development; for the first time the borders between the various storeys of the façade are clearly visible. Although the front serliana appears in a simplified form, a ledge projects from the foundations of the wall at the side of the round arch which leads around the loggia and meets its counterpart, where motifs are concerned, in the upper ends of the windows. A double ledge runs below the windows and connects the loggia organically with the rest of the building. Apart from its structural function, it forms both the upper and lower conclusions of two balusters, which are positioned among the outer pilasters of the serliana. If one also takes into consideration the fact that the balusters visually balance out the difference in height between the windows of the piano nobile and the outer pilasters of the serliana, then the Villa Forni-Cerato appears as a building in which the subordination of individual façade details with regard to the entire façade, which was characteristic of Palladio's later development, is expressed for the first time.

Above left: as at the Villa Godi, the steps, which lead up to the loggia of the Villa Forni-Cerato, reach above the basement. The staircase has a single flight and in its width corresponds to the width of the middle serlian opening.

Above right: reliefs which represent the two river gods are set into the two areas over the outer openings of the serliana. Both reliefs are twentieth century copies.

p. 31: an old copperplate engraving shows the Villa Forni-Cerato decorated with rich stucco-work. This decoration was removed at the beginning of the twentieth century. Only the mask over the arch of the entrance serliana still bears witness to the decoration, the work of Alessandro Vittoria.

Villa Gazotti

Bertesina (Vicenza)

The external form of the villa, which today is in a rather neglected condition, shows the person who commissioned it to have been a man who wanted to make his affluence clearly visible. He also possessed such a fortune that he was able to lead a life of leisure. For the first time Palladio presents the body of the building as a clearly defined cube. The three-fold arcade in the central section, which is reminiscent of the Villa Godi, is crowned by a triangular gable and is the dominant shape of the façade. It is less the embodiment of an original body of thought of Palladio's – comparable examples can be found both in the Villa Agostini in Cusignana di Arcade and in the architecture of Giovanni Maria Falconetto – than of his endeavour to give existing forms a new expression. What is new is that the three-fold arcade takes up the entire height of the one-storey building. Equally, the use in secular architecture of a triangular gable as a symbol of dignity has no counterpart in Venetian architecture of that time. A wide flight of steps was originally meant to lead up to the loggia; the narrow flight of steps which now leads up to the centre arcade in the loggia is a later addition.

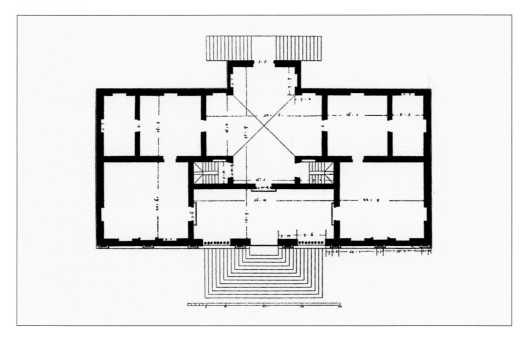

The ground-plan of the Villa Gazotti – a drawing by Francesco Muttoni – shows the method that was used to overcome the preconditions of the type of the two-towered villa: a loggia that protracts is interposed between the two protruding corner compartments, and its use means that the building can be seen as a nearly regular cuboid.

Detail of the pilasters. Composite capitals – in other words, capitals formed by the merging of the Ionic and Corinthian orders – form the upper conclusions of the pilasters and carry a multiple offset and variously-terraced entablature.

The windows of the Villa Gazotti are fitted with ledges. Above the window lintels, strongly protruding gables project from the stone work. Scroll-work supports, which carry the gable, are interposed between the differing levels of the reliefs.

The Villa Gazotti was in a rather neglected state for a long time. Recently, however, attempts have been made to restore the building to its former condition.

The body of the building rests on a base, from which it is divided by means of a ledge which runs along the entire width of the façade. On the one hand this serves to protect the working areas from damp, but on the other hand it also raises the villa above the surrounding landscape. This possibility of giving the building a prominent position was already made use of before Palladio by Falconetto, who placed the Villa Vescovile in Luvigliano, which was begun in 1534, on a heavily rusticated base.

Along with this adoption of contemporary architectural thinking, the Villa Gazotti also shows what in Venetia was a totally new way of treating wall surfaces. It is not the closed parts of the façade, but the open loggia which takes up the dominating position on the villa's façade. Beyond this, the way in which Palladio treats his façade makes it clearly recognisable that it is his intention to give the wall surfaces a plastic structure. Eight pilasters with composite capitals that project gently from the surface of the wall divide the façade into eight vertical rhythms. At the same time, the central part distinguished by its three-fold arcade is offset slightly from the rest of the façade. The windows are connected firmly to the body of the building by means of a lower window ledge which runs along the entire width of the façade and is offset along with the pedestals of the pilasters. In contrast to the Villa Godi and the Villa Piovene, the windows are no longer merely perforations in the wall, but through their plastic profiles and the protruding triangular gables at their tops have become independent structural elements on the Villa Gazotti's façade.

Even though Palladio endeavoured to open up the wall, which is usually seen as a border, it should not be overlooked that the façade of the Villa Gazotti still has a lot of unshaped wall surface above the windows. Nonetheless, the multiple layering of the wall by means of the arrangement of pilasters, window profiles and triangular gables is a clear indication that Palladio is now endeavouring to model and shape the massive body of the building derived from Venetian two-towered buildings through the use of a plastic structure and wide openings.

Villa Pisani

Bagnolo di Lonigo (Vicenza)

The Villa Pisani was built after 1542 in the town of Bagnolo, only a few kilometres away from the Vicenzan palace of Lonigo. In his *Quattro Libri*, Palladio names Vittore, Marco and Daniele Pisani as its owners. Because of an evaluation of the property which dates back to 1544, we can assume that the villa was nearly ready to be occupied at that time, or that the mansion at least had been finished. Palladio once again worked on the Villa Pisani around 1560: the farm wings were built then. The property lies on the river Gua and had belonged to the Pisani family since the 1520s. The Pisanis had been members of the nobility since 1523. In that year Giovanni Pisani acquired his title and the control of Bagnolo.

A palace-like villa already existed on the property by the Gua before the Villa Pisani was built, but it had been destroyed by fire. A small mediaeval fort is also spoken of in connection with the earlier building, which Palladio wanted to allude to in his new building.

Palladio himself describes the villa, whose planning stages had been extremely complicated, fully in his four books on architecture. One matter of secondary importance which he considers to be especially noteworthy is that "attention was not paid to situating the smaller flight of steps in a place which, as I recommended in my first book, would have sunlight falling on it, as the sole purpose of these steps is to lead to the rooms above and below, which are used as grain stores or mezzanine floors." At this point we are given the opportunity to understand an aspect of Palladio's thinking: one might conclude from what is said above that the Villa Pisani consisted of three storeys. But it does not do so in Palladio's sense. He only counts those floors as storeys that serve as living quarters for master and mistress. So while the Villa Pisani has a basement, piano nobile and mezzanine storey, to Palladio's way of thinking it is a one-storey building.

This way of dividing the storeys, in connection with the description cited above, also tells us that the Villa Pisani was thought of as being a functional agricultural building that should also offer its noble owners – the Pisanis were counts – the comforts of a life befitting their rank.

p. 35: Villa Pisani, Bagnolo. Ground-plan and elevation from the Quattro Libri. The estate was meant to have a function as an agricultural building. The cultivation of rice and hemp must have been very profitable. These riches resulted in the greatness of the courtyard, which no longer exists today. The farming wings would have surrounded an area the size of St. Mark's Square.

The connection of usefulness and comfort is made clear by the plan of the estate as published in the *Quattro Libri*: the villa lies at the lower end of a courtyard surrounded by farm wings. So-called "barchesses" – closed peristyles – at the front were intended to make it possible for the masters to reach every part of the estate without getting wet when it was raining. Stables and grain stores were incorporated in the farm wings. In this one-storey lay-out of the Villa Pisani, Palladio kept to one of Leon Battista Alberti's requirements, for the latter stressed at the end of the fifteenth century that there was absolutely no need to build several storeys in the country, as there was enough room to spread out across the ground. Indeed, according to Michelangelo Muraro, the farm wings enclose an area that is at least the size of the Piazza San Marco.

Today only the mansion house remains; the farm wings fell into ruin in the course of time. The mansion house itself shows once again, next

pp. 36/37: the Villa Pisani lies on the small river Gua. Its façade, which faces the river, took on the representation of the power of the Pisani family. The hinted-at towers, along with the rusticated round arches, tell of the might of this noble family.

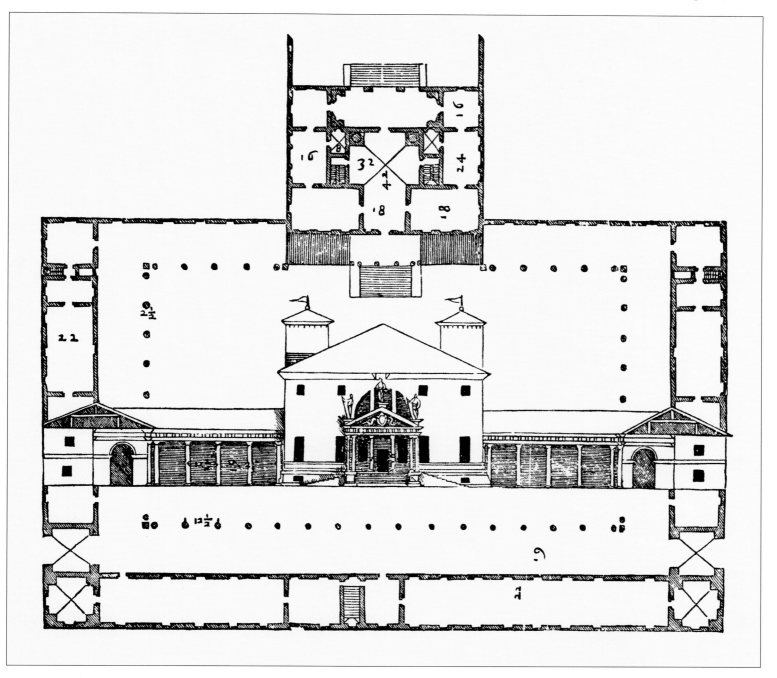

to the application of contemporary architectural theory, the commitment to the Venetian tradition of laying out villas that Palladio still felt in 1542: the façade facing the river has the appearance of a two-tower lay-out. The power of the Pisanis will certainly have played a part in Palladio's decision to make use once again of this type of villa. The river Gua which flows past the Villa Pisani was navigable, and the façade which faces the river had a public character. But when one looks at this façade one cannot help suspecting that the use of its individual parts cannot be explained merely by the meaning inherent in them. Certainly the two towers represent the power the Pisani family had in Bagnolo; this representation is not conveyed by the height of the towers, though. They rise above the cuboid body of the building to only an insignificant degree. Rather, the mezzanine storey of the courtyard façade is missing on the side of the villa facing the river. Connected merely by a triglyph ledge, the three-fold arcade ends directly in a mighty triangular gable. So it is less the existing towers that take on the representation of a well-fortified building than the appearance that the recessed loggia is flanked by two towers.

The rusticated triple arch arrangement is similarly mannerist. If one looks at this arcature independently of the rest of the building, one discovers that it is laid out in a perfectly artistic manner. Six pilasters of the Tuscan order are formed out of the rustication in this exciting play of light and shadow. There are two of these pilasters on the pillars on either side of the triple arch arrangement, while the two inner pillars are each defined by one pilaster. It is easy to see, however, that the rustication is applied as a deception, which is not even continued around the pillars, for even their sides are already smoothly plastered. However artistic the presentation of the loggia's shape is, it is added to the body of the building in a most inorganic way. It is indisputable that the rustication of the loggia is also an architectural documentation of a claim to power. But equally indisputable is the fact that the river façade of the Villa Pisani is a façade with a public character intended to convey status, which does not deliver architecturally what it promises visually.

A view of the courtyard façade shows what was typical of Palladio in these years, a pattern of windows as a geometrical arrangement to provide surface interest. As on the façade facing the river, the accentuation of the central axis cannot be overlooked on the courtyard façade. This accentuation is achieved by choosing an odd vertical rhythm, whose effect is heightened still further by the thermal window in the centre of the façade, which forms a too big vertical module along with the entrance portal and the two windows immediately next to it. The effect which can be felt even in the present condition would have been expressed even more clearly, had the four-column portico been carried out on the courtyard façade.

p. 39: the Pisani family performed their official duties in the great room. The frescoes in the roof vaulting date from the sixteenth century. The thermal window on the façade facing the garden was originally meant to have a counterpart on the river side. The mighty gable, however, ruled this out.

Palazzo and Villa Thiene

Palladian research has always made heavy weather of allocating the Palazzo Thiene a place in the stylistic development of Andrea Palladio's creative work. But questions as to his being the author do not pose any problem. This palace is described in Palladio's architectural treatise, where there are several illustrations of it.

In the case of the Palazzo Thiene we must also accept the fact that it was carried out only in part. Only two adjoining palace wings were built. Four were planned, and would have surrounded a courtyard of imposing size. But even that part of the plan that was carried out makes it possible for us to guess at the size the Palazzo Thiene would have been.

A different residence of the Thiene family originally stood in the grounds on which the Palazzo was built. Documents tell of a palace building that must evidently have been completed in 1495. But shortly after it was completed the loggia collapsed. Altough repair work was frequently undertaken on this palace building, in 1542 Marcantonio Thiene, the original builder's grandson, planned a new building which Andrea Palladio was to translate into action.

In his treatise, Palladio describes the position of the palace as being like an island. This marvellous monument was not of course supposed to be lapped by water; just the opposite: it was possible to put the cellar rooms below ground level, "as this building lies in the highest part of the town, where there is no danger of water causing trouble" (Andrea Palladio). On the other hand, Palladio must have felt the fact that the palace was to be bordered by four streets to be as it were insular. In addition, one of the four façades would have faced onto "the loveliest street in the city", and the palace would have furthermore been situated near the main square in Vicenza – the Piazza dei Signori, which was the administrative centre of the city for many centuries.

As the palace was to be situated in such an imposing position, one might expect richly structured façades to tell of the rank of the palace's owner. Just the opposite is the case: the building appears to be extremely massive, and the completed palace would have reminded one of a modified form of a Roman castrum. The rusticated piantereno

"This house is in the centre of the town near the main square, which is why it seemed useful to me to include some shops on the side towards the main square, as the architect has to consider what is to the advantage of the client, where-space permits. Every shop has a separate room above for the dealers, and above these are the masters' rooms. This house is situated almost as if on an island, being surrounded by four streets. The main entrance, or rather the main gate, has a loggia built in front of it and allows access to the liveliest street in the town . . . The cellars and similar rooms are below ground level, as this building stands in the highest part of the town, where there is no danger of water causing any problems."
(Andrea Palladio, 1570)

rises immediately from ground level. The rustication is carried out in a monotonous fashion. The monotonous sequence of the layering of stone blocks is interrupted only above the windows. The windows themselves make the impression of having been cut out of the mighty stone work. Smoothly plastered blind arches are set above the windows, and are surrounded almost protectively by round arches. These round arches are formed, as is the entire piantereno, out of rusticated stone blocks. They do not, however, project out of the wall, but are incorporated in the rest of the rustication. Stonework that is trapezoid and therefore divides out in a star shape starts above the window lintels and cuts into the blind arches. This artistic device is the only decorative form to brighten up the façade of the piantereno.

The visual claim of the Palazzo Thiene to be an example of fortress architecture finds its correlation in the piano nobile. The piano nobile is rusticated, as is the piantereno, however in a kind of rustication that is more moderate than that of the piantereno.

The piano nobile is livened up to a certain extent by the regular alternation of triangular and segmental arch gables. Nevertheless the piano nobile too appears to be unusually massive. On the façades of other palaces by Palladio can be seen the architect's endeavours to fill

Right: ground-plan and elevation of the Palazzo Thiene from the Quattro Libri. The Palazzo Thiene is one of Palladio's first commissions of public and town representation. In its architecture, Palladio alludes to the military tradition of his client. Only two of the planned four wings on the sketch were actually built.

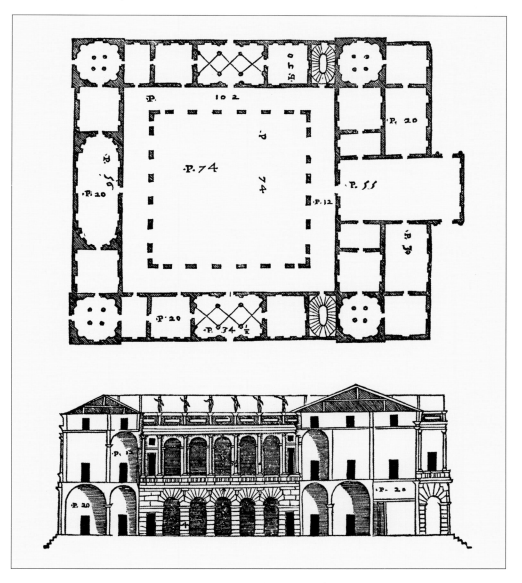

pp. 42/43: not much remains in the courtyard façades of the massive unity of the street façades of the Palazzo Thiene. A two-storey loggia opens onto the courtyard in wide arch arrangements.

M·ANTONIVS·THIENALVS·IO·GALEAT

up the empty, undecorated wall surfaces with decorative work; on the façade of the Palazzo Thiene, however, the opposite path is taken. The windows are drawn down right to the ledge, so that the latter serves in addition as the windows' ledge.

Consoles project strongly in a regular sequence from the sides of the windows, and in using this motif Palladio makes no effort to conceal the sympathy for the formal properties of Giulio Romano that he surely possessed.

However, we cannot simply disregard the form of the window frames. On closer inspection, we see that a narrow Ionic entablature leads around the palace façade at the height of the window lintels. In accordance with Renaissance building logic, such an entablature must be supported by corresponding Ionic columns; the search for them is difficult, but not hopeless: we find them in front of the sides of the windows, as supports of the projecting window lintels, but well-hidden by the consoles described above.

That columns should be covered in a rusticated casing was not uncommon practice in the time around 1545; but this was done by a rusticated band which was suited to the round shape of the columns. Here, however, on the façade of the Palazzo Thiene, two opposed forms work against each other in a battle which the round shape of the columns clearly loses.

Above left: the Palazzo Thiene conveys a rather massive impression, which is created by the uniform rough rusticated squares of the lower storey and the extensive unadorned wall surfaces of smooth rustication in the piano nobile. Because the two completed wings of the palace border the edges of two narrow streets, their street façades cannot be visually appreciated in their entirety.

Above right: the Palazzo Thiene was taken over by the Banca Popolare in 1872. Extensive renovation work was done, including the internal arrangement of the building. Changes were also made on the façade.

We can interpret this in two ways which are not mutually exclusive. On the one hand, there is the fortified character of the palace. Its protective function evidently also reaches to the columns, which are surrounded by rustication as if by a protective casing. On the other, it should not be overlooked that such a process adapts the round shape of the columns to the smooth, angular elements which structure the façade. The vertical structure of the piano nobile takes place through the use of pilasters which function as a visible sign of the supporting elements that have been used. The arrangement of pilasters is determined by a regular pattern.

As can be seen generally in Palladio's work, here too the palace ground-plan becomes apparent on the façade. A look at this ground-plan shows that rooms on an octagonal ground-plan were meant to be added to the four corners of the palace. Palladio mentions these in his descriptions as rooms that are extremely pleasant on account of their very shape.

This prominent position of the rooms is also visible on the palace's façade: their windows are sided by arrangements of double pilasters, which additionally take on the function of strengthening the corners of the palace. The solution for the treatment of the façade which is found for the piano nobile is definitely successful and original. The surrounding Ionic entablature divides the area of the façade over the piantereno into two storeys, thereby making the pilasters, which support the Attic entablature, overlap the storeys, or to be more precise, giving them a colossal character.

The rhythm caused by the pilasters and the regular alternation of triangular and segmental arch gables crowning the windows is nonetheless opposed by an extremely massive façade impression. The formation of a sham storey by the Ionic entablature on the one hand legitimises what is at first sight an exceedingly disproportionate pattern of windows in the piano nobile. On the other hand, an empty space is created, which is not filled by any decorative work or given a function by the addition of a mezzanine storey. This enables the square stonework of the wall to make a full impact.

This impression of isolation has its counterpart in the ground-plan of the palace.

Characterized by a regular quadrangular base, it displays four self-

Below: ground-plan and elevation of the Villa Thiene from the Quattro Libri. The drawing that was published in the architectural treatise can hardly claim to represent the building. Palladio published an idealised plan of the project, which had already been at a standstill for many years.

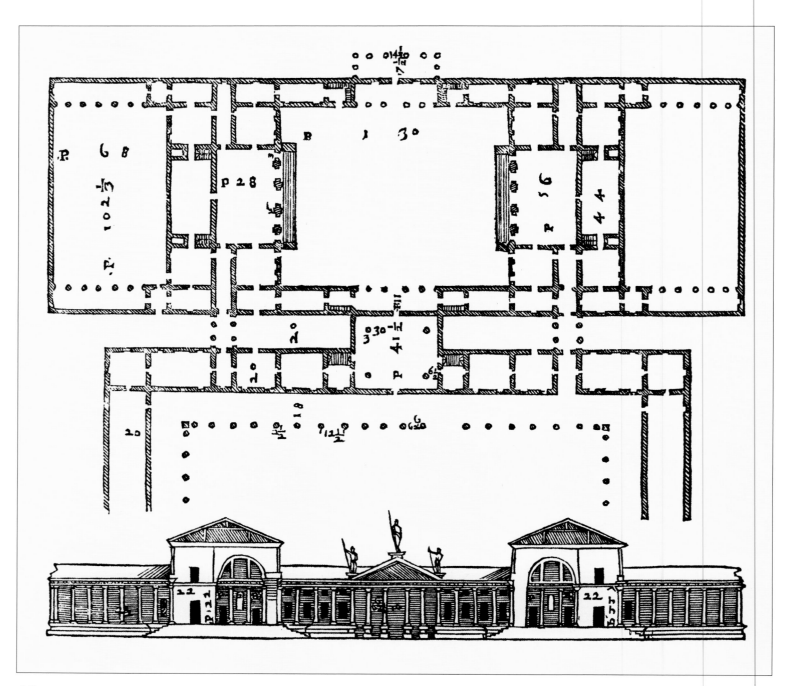

contained rows of rooms which are connected to each other by the risalito-like corner rooms, which have already been discussed.

Distinctions can nevertheless be made. The task of attesting status would have fallen to that palace wing which would have bordered the main street. In contrast to the three remaining wings of the palace, it is not characterized by a simple row of rooms; two layers of rooms are placed one in front of the other, linked by a vestibule which would have appeared on the façade in the shape of a risalito. The foremost, which is evidently to be considered bordered by regular arch arrangements, would have yielded to a loggia. Shops were to be incorporated in the row of rooms behind the loggia. So that wing of the palace which would have had to convey the message of status would at the same time have been as it were the public part of the palace. The front loggia does not continue on the other sides. So the three remaining palace wings would only have been characterized by a simple row of rooms with no further layer of rooms in front of them. But in their structure they correspond to the room lay-out of the main façade, which had the function of being a row of shops. In each case it is the central rooms that have the greatest volume; the bordering rooms are organized in their development towards this centre from the smallest up to the largest room.

The self-contained room lay-outs present the palace wings as each being autonomous components of the palace lay-out and reinforce in the interior what is already expressed on the façade: that the Palazzo Thiene is a case of a bastion that is closed off to the outside and all sides, and that apart from its function of providing a place to live it also takes on one of defence.

How, though, should such architecture in the centre of a town be explained? The answer to this question must start with the political position of Vicenza around 1540. The town which lay on the Terraferma was under the control of Venice's administration. The times were however anything but rosy for Venice. The roots of this crisis reach right back to the end of the fourteenth century. In order to protect itself from the threat of the mainland provinces, Venice had begun to enlarge its sphere of influence on the Terraferma. This policy of expansion was also aimed at safeguarding the trade routes there. The process of annexation had largely been completed by 1405. Vicenza was one of the towns which were now under the control of the government of the Serenissima. The annexations that had occurred were welcomed by the country's people; from now on, not only did the administration of these towns lie in the hands of Venice, but Venice also controlled its members.

The local nobility was not only excluded from politics, but the Venetian administration also protected the rural population from its interference. This understandably irritated the nobility considerably. But it was not only the humiliatingly ignored noblemen who watched Venice's expansion with uneasiness; the mainland provinces also took an extremely sceptical view of Venice's policy of expansion, as they were afraid that Venice would extend its territory further and further. Prompted by the Duke of Mantua and supported by Pope Julius II, a

pp. 48/49: the present main façade of the Villa Thiene acquired its current appearance in the nineteenth century. At that time, the great portal in the centre of the façade was broken into the stone-work. This façade was probably not that of the mansion but of one of the agricultural wings.

47

Holy League was formed towards the end of the fifteenth century, which some Italian dukedoms, the Pope, as well as Louis XII of France, Maximilian I of Austria and Charles V of Spain took part in. The goal which they declared and resolved upon at Cambrai in 1509 was that of putting an end to the Serenissima and dividing up its possessions. Venice had to defend itself vigorously against this League between 1509 and 1513. And even when the League fell apart in 1513 because of internal differences, the fighting did not cease. But the policy which had been shown the local nobility of the Terraferma had already been avenged and had repeatedly led to disloyal behaviour.

Wars cost a lot of money at any time, and even Venice's financial sources were nearly threatening to run dry. In addition, the discovery of a sea route to India by the Portuguese Vasco da Gama caused Venice's monopoly on the spice trade to begin to falter. Due to the Treaties of Brussels of 1517, Venice could at least see its possessions on the Terraferma confirmed. In the meantime, lessons had been learnt from the bad administrative policies of past years: the local nobility was included in Venice's policy for the Terraferma. The importance of the towns on the Terraferma for the Republic on the lagoon was also considered, both in military and economic respect. Many Venetians began to invest their money by buying land on the Terraferma, thereby laying the foundation for the phenomenon of the country residence.

But the awareness of the military importance of the mainland for Venice also produced consequences. In connection with this it should not be overlooked that already at that time it was cannon that determined conflicts and in the case of Venice also led to its defeats. So they had to set about fortifying the towns accordingly.

First endeavours were translated into action by the architect Fra Giocondo as early as 1510 in Treviso. After 1517 these endeavours increased, and applied not only to the town walls but to the palaces also. The architect Michele Sanmicheli was a pioneer of such an action, and his frequent use of massive rustication definitely became a characteristic style.

So it is not surprising that in the Palazzo Thiene we see a town palace which in the massive way it is built and its monumental proportions appears to share the characteristics of fortress architecture. Thirty years had passed since the Treaties of Brussels, though. Venice's interest in a fortified mainland was however as great as before, and Marcantonio Thiene's palace project fits in with these interests as the project of a commissioning builder who was raised to the nobility in 1523 by Venice, although his father had been disloyal to Venice and had lived in exile in Mantua during Venice's clashes with the League of Cambrai.

That it was not to be merely a pure manifestation of loyalty, but that the massive architecture of the Palazzo Thiene was in its way to constitute to a high degree a representation of Marcantonio Thiene's power, is without doubt. His endeavour to make power and status visually effective in architecture resulted in a further project which Palladio was to plan for Marcantonio Thiene: the building of a villa in

p. 51: detail of a window in the piano nobile of the Palazzo Thiene. In this picture we see clearly what can only be seen with difficulty when walking past. The cornices, which frame the window, surround columns of the Ionic order. All the same, Palladio puts the volutes of the capitals cross-wise over them, probably in order not to completely conceal them from any spectators strolling along the street.

Quinto. The commission must have been awarded around 1546, at a time when the work on the town palace was in full swing. The Thiene family were rich merchants, whose prosperity originated among other things from the trade in silk. Giangaleazzo, Marcantonio's father, took part additionally in the improvement of the swamplands of the Terraferma. A property of the Thiene family in Quinto, on which a new villa was to be built, dates from this time.

Here too Palladio is proven as the author by his architectural treatise, although the published drawing can hardly be reconciled with the actual villa project. History teaches us on the contrary that the impression that the present façade of the Villa Thiene is the main façade is a very deceptive one. Both the mighty gable and the portal are alterations to the building dating from the nineteenth century. That which today presents itself as the main façade was originally only a side façade, which also had to be completed in a stately fashion, as it faced the river Tesina which flowed past.

We can only infer Palladio's actual intentions from drawings by the architect Francesco Muttoni. In 1740 he was given the task of completing the villa, at any rate in part. The original project, which he records in drawings, appears to have been adapted from the Villa Gazotti-Marcello. The plan of two mansions lying opposite each other that was intended in the *Quattro Libri* must have been seen as highly utopian, though. The planning of only one mansion, even as a lay-out of two separate living quarters as described by Muttoni, can be seen to be much more likely.

The villa in Quinto was meant to have huge dimensions, just like the Thiene family's town palace. Both projects must have been based on an exceptional ambition on the part of its commissioners, an ambition which did however cause Marcantonio Thiene to overestimate his financial resources. In his urge to give expression to his status he had gone too far. Soon after the building had been begun, the work on the villa already came to a standstill. Marcantonio Thiene evidently tried to make that part of the villa which had already been completed ready for occupation. So he had the artist Giovanni Indemio provide some rooms with frescoes. A short time after the building in Quinto was stopped, the work on the town palace in Vicenza also had to be discontinued.

When Marcantonio Thiene died in 1558, he left his son Ottavio two fragments of buildings, which the latter was evidently not willing to complete. Documents do however testify to the fact that he thought of having a garden laid out, in the centre of which there was to be a labyrinth. As has already been mentioned, another attempt to continue the building of the villa was made around 1740. Muttoni's interventions altered the project decisively. But even after that the Villa Thiene was at the mercy of alterations, so that merely the northern front of the Villa Thiene can be seen as being Palladio's work, although it is made unfamiliar and given a new meaning by the gable and portal. Like the Tower of Babel, both of Marcantonio Thiene's monumental projects had fallen through because of the excessive ambition of their builder.

"Once these matters have been taken into account, both in the plan and in the model, one should calculate the costs, carefully, and see to the availability of money in good time, as well as the necessary building materials, so that nothing will delay or prevent completion of the construction work once building has been begun. The builder will find it of no small advantage if his walls are put up with due speed, all in the same style and at the same time, and are not cracked as buildings are that have been completed over various periods and without any consistency in the work." (Andrea Palladio, 1570)

Above: the garden façade of the Villa Thiene can be attributed to Francesco Muttoni. Both the thermal window in the concluding gable and portals in the centre part of the façade are displeasing. These elements cannot be reconcited with Palladio's formal idiom.

Villa Saraceno

Finale di Agugliano (Vicenza)

Not dissimilar to the Villa Forni-Cerato in form and appearance, the Villa Saraceno lies on an artificially raised area on the banks of the Liona Canal in Finale di Agugliano, a town near Vicenza. If one is willing to give credence unreservedly to Andrea Palladio's *Quattro Libri*, then the Villa Saraceno must have been an excellent estate, upon which the ravages of time have performed their sorry work, leaving a mansion house which has only one of the agricultural buildings remaining. For the drawing in Palladio's architectural treatise presents an estate with a dominating mansion house in its centre, flanked on both sides by farming wings which close like arms around the estate's courtyard. Two cylindrical towers at the corners of the farming wings should also be mentioned.

There is no doubt that Biagio Saraceno was the client for whom it was built. He held important offices, and was one of the patriarchs of Vicenza. Although this has not been proved by records, it can be assumed with a high degree of likelihood that the villa was built around 1545. The year 1560 marks the extension of the estate by some landholdings. In the relevant document of 31st January 1560 it is also mentioned that this piece of land bordered Biagio Saraceno's domicile. This domicile must also have already existed in 1552, the year in which Biagio Saraceno's right of ownership to the property, which he had inherited from his father, was confirmed. This villa, that to all appearances had been completed, is revealed by Palladio's description in the *Quattro Libri* to be an agriculturally functional building. As a protection against flood water from the Liona Canal, the level of the floor of the rooms was raised by five Vicenzan feet over the area which had anyway already been artificially raised. The position of the villa on a river did justice to Palladio's requirement, which saw an advantage in a position by a navigable stretch of water if just in the possibility of shipping agricultural goods. Everything was geared to utility, even inside the building.

The outer appearance of the mansion most readily conforms with the design and description. In a simple formal idiom typical of Palladio's early work, a risalito dominates as the accentuation of the central part of the building, is closed off at the top by a triangular gable

"The mansion house was built: but the annexes are missing which would have completed Palladio's invention. The kitchens and other working rooms, the porticos, stables, agricultural areas were not even begun: and it was added to as necessary, either with buildings that already existed or by later ones."
Ottavio Bertotti-Scamozzi, 1778

pp. 56/57: *"But a nobleman will obtain not inconsiderable use and relaxation from the villa, where he spends the rest of his time both keeping an eye on his possessions and perfecting them, and letting his wealth grow by diligence and the aid of the science of agriculture." (Andrea Palladio, 1570)*

and is broken up by a three-fold arcature. A wide flight of steps leads up to the loggia and emphasises the dominating position of the latter. Two vertical rows of windows stand in agreement with the loggia, and make clear the division into storeys of the villa. The windows of the piano nobile are more strongly profiled than the mezzanine windows and in addition have a triangular gable as their upper conclusion.

The first inconsistency with the drawing in Palladio's architectural treatise appears in the unfortunate relationship to each other of the arch arrangement, architrave and gable of the building as it was carried out. This imbalance was altered to be classically correct in the drawing published in 1570. However, the inside of the villa also shows up inconsistencies. They struck the architect Francesco Muttoni in 1740. Ottavio Bertotti-Scamozzi is even more clear, for he reports in 1778 that neither the kitchens nor the farming wings then existed. People built according to the need of the moment or extended an existing building. So we now on the one hand have the description in Palladio's architectural treatise, and on the other the statements of two contemporaries of the eighteenth century, which contradict the former. Lionello Puppi offers a plausible solution to the problem in his detailed monograph on Palladio; he suspects that the texts in the *Quattro Libri* were brought into line with each other with the intention of bringing out a textbook.

Below: ground-plan and elevation of the Villa Saraceno from the Quattro Libri. The client, Biagio Saraceno, was principally interested in the profitable aspect of the villa. The façade can most easily be brought into accord with Palladio's design. The plan underwent drastic changes in the interior of the villa. An architect of the eighteenth century established that the villa had evidently been built merely in accordance with the immediate requirements.

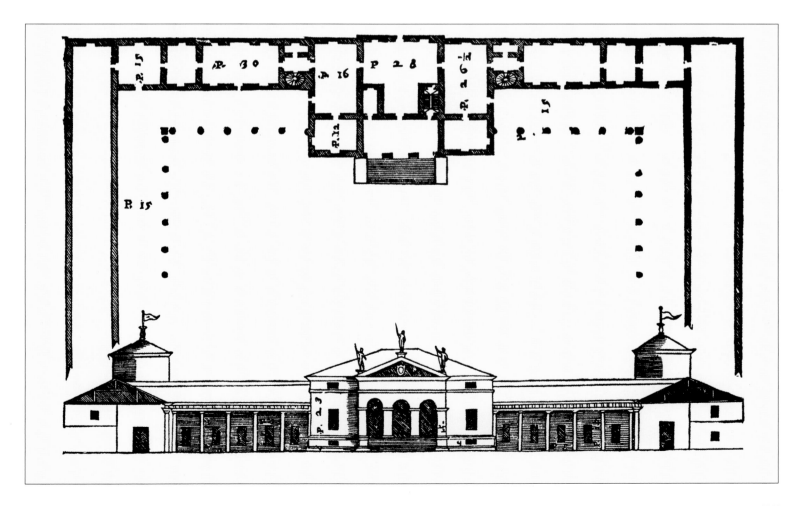

Villa Poiana

Poiana Maggiore (Vicenza)

Bonifacio Poiana commissioned Andrea Palladio to build a country seat in Poiana Maggiore near Vicenza between 1548 and 1549. Bonifacio Poiana came of a family with a knightly tradition and close commitments to soldiering. He had behaved absolutely loyally towards the Republic of Venice during the war against the League of Cambrai, and now, in the "Pax Venezia", joined in the developing of the Terraferma and devoted himself to agriculture. The estate with which Palladio had been commissioned had to meet two conditions: on the one hand the architecture was meant to display the position and tradition of the Poiana family; on the other hand the estate was meant to be agriculturally useful.

The solution which Palladio presented is one of the most beautiful of his buildings. Situated on a hill top, the Villa Poiana attracts attention to its simple shape. Its proportions are well-balanced: the sections of the two main façades relate to each other in a 1:2:1 ratio.

Below: ground-plan and elevation of the Villa Poiana from the Quattro Libri. Only the mansion in the sketch was built during Palladio's lifetime. Bonifacio Poiana's interest in his estate obviously mainly concerned its aspect as a place of relaxation. Correspondingly, the first parts of the estate to be completed were those which served the purpose of leisure.

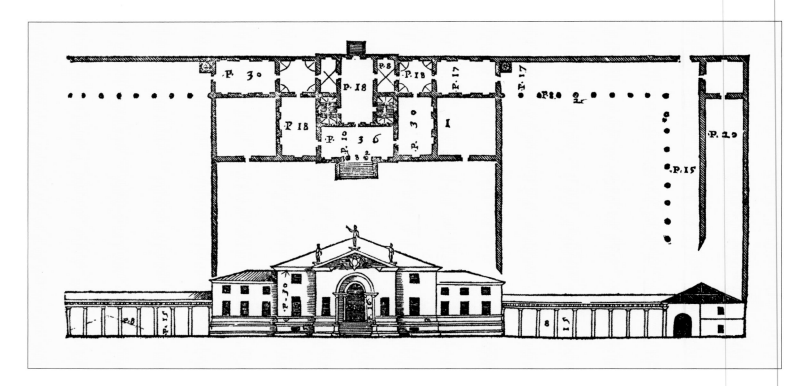

Michelangelo Muraro remarked, not without good reason, that this causes the building to look smaller than it really is. Once again it is the gently protruding risalito-like central part of the building that dominates due to being slightly offset from the façade. In this risalito a motif is carried out with which Palladio had already experimented in early drawings of plans for villas: that of the broken gable. Because the console ledge is broken into, it has been organically fused with the wall surface of the risalito. A simple serliana dominates both on the front and rear façades. Palladio here presents this motif with a remarkable variation, for he makes it project into a double round arch which encloses five oculi. Supported by the two windows at the sides of the serliana, the latter stands in direct relationship with the broken gable, thereby resolving the classical portico motif, constituting an arch arrangement, architrave and gable, in favour of an organic fusion of the elements.

The Villa Poiana dispenses with any form of decoration. The ser-

liana makes the impression of being as it were cut into the stonework, its supports being simple, smoothly plastered pillars. The lower window ledges merge only weakly offset into a surrounding ledge and merely the upper conclusions of the windows project more strongly from the stonework. This rejection of ornamental forms corresponds to the military tradition of the Poiana family and is rooted in a building tradition which expresses its well-fortified condition by doing without the "decoro".

Nonetheless, the Villa Poiana was part of a development which came from the peaceful atmosphere which now prevailed, and in many places caused architects to draw up an open type of architecture, in contrast to closed-off, massive buildings. So in the Villa Poiana as well – and for the first time in Palladio's works – an exceptional openness of the rooms goes along with the simple treatment of the façade. This experience of space starts at the loggia. Because the portico does not protrude in front, the loggia is surrounded by the body of the building. As the living rooms are ordered like a suite to the left and right of a central axis, the view through the loggia is a view through the entire body of the building. In this way the Villa Poiana fits organically in with the surrounding countryside, indeed even becomes a firm component of this landscape.

The plasterwork of the Villa Poiana, even though it is now in bad

Above and p. 63 left: theme and variation: Palladio frequently included a serliana in the shaping of his façades, particularly in his early buildings, and this was therefore later also called the Palladio motif. Here it appears in an interesting variation: it projects into a double round arch, which surrounds five oculi (circular incisions in the stonework).

2" /›

Above right: an ancient scene of sacrifice by Anselmo Canera. The fresco in the main room of the villa alludes to its owner: a family is depicted, whose head is bringing the torch of war to be extinguished at the altar of peace.

condition, makes possible an observation which can also be made at the Villa Godi in Lonedo and the Villa Pisani in Montagnana: it displays a carved square pattern which is capable of giving the impression that the Villa Poiana is faced with smooth hewn stone. This method of treating the façade will have heightened the dignified character of the villa still further without disturbing the dialogue of the simple wall surfaces with the openings of the loggia and the windows.

As with many of Palladio's buildings, the history of the building of the Villa Poiana is one of complications. A document dating from 1555 says that the villa was not completed at that point. It must nevertheless already have been habitable, as the fresco decorations can be dated to 1550. However, neither the surrounding walls nor the flight of steps in front of the loggia were built until some time between the end of the sixteenth and middle of the seventeenth centuries. The extensions to the central part of the villa were also not built until this time, in which Francesco Muttoni was heeded little due to Palladio's design. A report by Filippo Pigafetta is informative, for according to it only that part of the villa that was meant for relaxation and improvement was built. It is perhaps not entirely unjustified to see in Bonifacio Poiana a commissioning client, to whom the surrounding landscape gave one more reason for joining in with the humanist ideal of a life in the country.

Palazzo della Ragione

Piazza dei Signori (Vicenza)

Palladio established his reputation with the so-called basilica, in reality the two-storeyed loggias, with which the older Palazzo Pubblico or Palazzo della Ragione (i. e. the town hall) was surrounded. His friendship with the poet and scholar Giangiorgio Trissino may have played a decisive part in Palladio's being awarded the contract. On 6th March 1546, Giovanni da Pedemuro together with his student Andrea Palladio presented a new project within this complicated history of planning. According to the wording of the document, an "almost life-size" model was to be made. It is possible that this meant the building of a single accurate scale arch, as in the building history of other important monuments. On 27th October of the same year, Palladio alone was commissioned to make four drawings of the building. The work on carrying them out was assigned to him on 11th April 1549 and his appointment as the chief architect followed on 1st May.

The work dragged on slowly, continually delayed by financial crises. By 23rd July 1561 the nine ground floor arcades facing the Piazza dei Signori, the four bordering ones on the narrow west side and the single one intended for the east side had been completed. The decision to carry out the upper loggia did not follow until 6th March 1564. Palladio did not live to see the building completed. The last payments are recorded as having been made on 14th March 1617. The completion of the sculptural ornamentation dragged on into the middle of the seventeenth century.

Palladio bases his concept on the principle of the walls of ancient Roman theatres: the vertical axes are structured by equal openings in the various storeys and by half-columns in front of them, the horizontals are accentuated by ledges, which are offset around the shapes on the walls. This principle is enriched by the use of the serliana, which is the connection, like a triumphal arch, of a central wide arch arrangement with two architraved, that is horizontally closed, passages, and which had previously been used to this extent only in Giulio Romano's Palazzo del Te in Mantua (1526–34).

Sebastiano Serlio (1475–1554), who at his time had emerged less as an architect than as an architectural theoretician, and in his seven books on architecture published from 1537 onwards had given the

"Just as the ancients built their basilicas in order for people to have a place, both in winter and summer, where they could negotiate their affairs and deals in comfort, so we, in our own time, build some public rooms in every Italian town, which can rightly be called basilicas, as the municipal authorities are accommodated quite close to them . . ."
(Andrea Palladio, 1570)

pp. 66/67: *the term "basilica", with which Palladio described the Palazzo della Ragione in Vicenza, has nothing in common with the type of church which has borne this name since early Christendom. Palladio was thinking of ancient buildings within which, he writes, "judges dispensed justice" and "now and again great and important matters were discussed."*

Below: Palazzo della Ragione. Ground-plan according to the Quattro Libri. That Palladio reproduces the ground-plan of the basilica in his treatise is somewhat misleading. His contribution to the building consisted in the construction of the loggias with which he surrounded the old core of the building. The openings of the blind arches are regular; however, both the ground-plan and the view of the façade show irregular spaces between the columns at the corner sections.

modern age what was up to that point the most comprehensive presentation of the teachings of Vitruvius, had used this motif familiar in Ancient Rome so frequently in the drawings added to his published books, that it was named after him, although it had already become established once more in the architecture of the fifteenth century. The alternate balance of horizontals and verticals, which characterizes the entire structure of the loggias, is in this way taken up and varied in each arch arrangement.

Palladio did not however make do with the traditional use of this motif, but projected it into the third dimension: the columns of the serliana are doubled on the inside of the loggia. In this way the round arch becomes a kind of narrow barrel vault and small flat-topped bays are created between the double columns and the bordering pilasters. While Giulio Romano had already solved the purpose of a loggia — as a connection between the inside and outside — in an almost ideal manner in Mantua, Palladio went one step further: in making the structured wall itself permeable, he actually raises the barrier between the arcade and the square. The oculi which are broken into the spandrels next to the round arches support this effect. Light and shadow are the essential elements in setting the inside and outside off against each other.

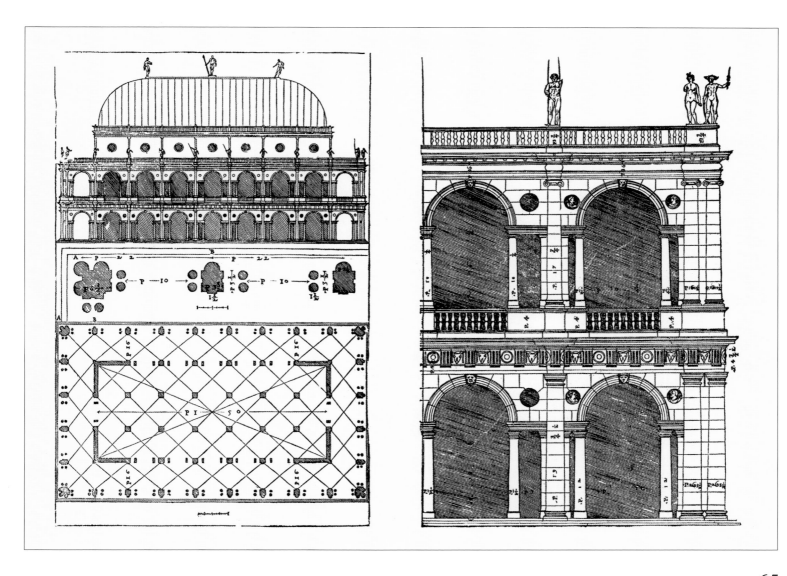

65

This new interpretation of the wall can be called Mannerist; for a phenomenon traditionally concerned with a certain task is turned into its very opposite. Nonetheless, the roots of this serliana carried into space seem to date back to the High Renaissance: an engraving by Marcanton Raimondi after Raphael's *Last Supper* shows a serliana as a window in the rear wall. It does not seem to be known in the architecture practised in Raphael's vicinity. But it became all the more amazingly widespread after Palladio. It appears in the upper storey of the Great Cloisters in the Convento do Cristo in Tomar (Portugal) which was begun in 1566 by Diego de Torralva and completed around 1580 by Filippo Terzi, and also in the model which Joseph Heintz created in 1609 for a hall on the Perlachplatz in Augsburg (Germany); and it even crosses the frontiers of art genres: in Veronese's painting *The Banquet in the House of Levi* (1573) in the Galleria dell'Accademia in Venice it constitutes the architecture in the foreground, though it stretches backwards.

If one has memorized the structure of the building, the whole of it seems to be characterized by the greatest simplicity: a dominant motif is repeated in both horizontal and vertical directions. The building does however acquire its fine rhythmical liveliness from a number of variations. In each case the outer axes are clearly contrasted: while the width of the arches corresponds to all the others, the architraved sides are considerably narrower. Altogether this results in an impression of contraction. Nonetheless these axes appear to be more massive, as there are no oculi in the arch spandrels there.

Altogether the accentuation of the corners works by means of a double column arrangement which is the equivalent of a pause: both in the upper and lower storeys the façade has the effect of being set in a firm frame, as it were.

In the loggia on the ground floor, Palladio uses the Doric order for both the great and small column arrangements, although with some fine differentiations: while the half-columns with their Attic bases (a sequence of torus, scotia and torus) strictly follow the Doric order, the added double columns appear in the variant of the so-called Tuscan order, a form which presumably came into being in Etruscan architecture, was taken over by Roman builders and was used once more especially in the sixteenth century: it rejects the Attic base in favour of a simple round base plate. Palladio proceeds in a similar fashion in the upper storey: in accordance with classical Roman usage, the great half-columns are formed in the Ionic order, whereby the volutes, which roll up at the sides, emphasize the association of the surfaces; in contrast, the added double columns stand on those same round bases that are contrasted only by a profile which makes the impression of being carved.

The profiles of the ledges and arches are closely related to each other. The arcade arches in both storeys are enlivened by so-called fascias, band-like three-layered profiles which become narrower lower down. These profiles, whether they project more or less plastically, also dominate the ledges above the arches and the architraves of the narrow side passages. Simultaneous consonance and variation

"Palladio's first great building was the so-called basilica in Vicenza, which was the surrounding of the mediaeval Palazzo della Ragione with two storeys of open arched halls, and in which he had annoyingly to take into account the structure of the wall (windows and other things) of the older building. Nonetheless – and despite individual details of great clumsiness in his own work – one of the most marvellous works of the sixteenth century came into being, which, for example, completely overshadows Sansovino's Biblioteca in Venice."
(Jacob Burckhardt, The Cicerone, 1855)

68

also characterizes the balustrades above each storey. While the side openings of the serliana are closed by a base in the central horizontal axis, and the round arch arrangement in contrast opens with a broken balustrade, the motif of the balustrade runs through to the top of the building, although made rhythmic: it not only takes up the way the great column order is offset, but emphasises each of the subordinated double columns on the vertical lines by closed rectangular areas. At the same time Palladio takes into account its function as the upper conclusion by making the ledge, which carries the balustrade, higher, more richly differentiated and above all by distinguishing it by means of a convex curved torus, which creates the impression of a soft springy cushion over the Ionic capitals.

In addition, Palladio emphasizes the concluding ledge by means of a console frieze. So the ledge and balustrade fulfil their function as the concluding building parts, but also lead across to the previously existing core of the Palazzo della Ragione: the blocks which crown the balustrade as concluding parts of the vertical architectural lines, serve at the same time as the pedestals for sculptures, which though they were not carried out while Palladio was still alive, were surely intended from the start inasmuch as they lead one's eyes up to the keel-shaped curved roof of the main building.

The oculi in the arch spandrels can also be viewed in the sense of connecting the older building with the nine two-storeyed loggias: as much as on the one hand they support the permeability of the wall, they equally have the function of being a link with the main building whose interior is lit by round windows.

Below: due to financial crises, the work on the basilica was delayed again and again. It is recorded that the last payments for the construction work were made in 1617, thirty-seven years after Palladio's death. The completion of the sculptural decoration even dragged on into the middle of the seventeenth century.

So Palladio's concept lives in the relationships of the parts to one another, without the impression of a similarity of shape being created. It is merely the architrave which separates the two storeys — being at the same time the upper conclusion of the ground storey loggias and the base of the upper arches — that is unique within the structure. Here Palladio takes up the motif of metope and triglyph friezes, that he had found both in Ancient Roman architecture and in that of the High Renaissance: there is an alternation in the relief of three carved rectangular areas (the triglyphs) followed by recessed squares, which are alternately decorated either with bulls' skulls between branches or with multiply profiled medallions (the metopes). So-called guttae, drop-like rows of ornamental elements, hang underneath the triglyphs, and also follow ancient models. The fact that the triglyphs and metopes close together over the great columns proves just how much Palladio here is still committed to a Mannerist style of thinking: the metopes reach around from the back to the block, whose front side had a reduced triglyph with only two notches. It is the only "unclear" aspect of the loggias' microstructure. Did Palladio intend a visual alignment of the right-angled block to the semi-circular columns, and was he willing to give up the exact delimitation of the individual architectural parts to achieve this? At any rate the linking of the individual elements is a basic principle of this architecture. The heads

Above left: at the corners of the basilica, the side openings of the serliana are somewhat smaller than in the rest of the loggia. In order to disguise this fact, Palladio only hints at the oculi in the spandrels, without letting them break up the stonework. Moreover, he strengthens the corners with additional columns.

Above right: the serlian motif originates in the ancient repertoire of forms. During the Renaissance, its use was spread, especially by Sebastiano Serlio. Palladio gave this motif a third dimension, by leading it backwards with a second column arrangement. The oculi in the spandrels date back to Palladio's knowledge of the Palazzo della Ragione which was built between 1420 and 1435.

in the tops of the arches of both storeys, which connect the semicircular and horizontal profiles with each other should be mentioned in connection with this.

Palladio's identification as the main architect of the basilica had been preceded by an extremely complicated history of construction. It was possible to complete the work on a new building of the Palazzo della Ragione by 1458, which in turn had to take older existing parts into consideration. The architect was presumably Domenico da Venezia. A lead-covered wooden roof truss was added between 1458 and 1460. The building of an arcade on the ground floor of the façade facing the Piazza dei Signori was first thought of two decades later. Eleven arch arrangements were planned. But the clients did not have much luck with their plans, as the work was brought to a halt by a cave-in in 1496. The respected architect and sculptor Antonio Rizzo was brought from Venice as an expert, and he recommended that what had been completed so far should be torn down to make way for a new building.

So Rizzo started the work again, but left Vicenza after a short time, so that Giorgio Spavento took over from him in 1498. Work will probably have been limited, as the war against France was straining the financial resources of the Republic of Venice.

All the same, resuming the project was considered in 1529–30, even before the Peace of Bologna. In the May of 1525, a report was obtained from the Venetian architect Antonio Abbondio, called Scarpagnino. He continued the work after 1532, but a short time later the work on the building was once again interrupted. In the following years the most distinguished architects in northern Italy were consulted: in 1538 Jacopo Sansovino – the first architect of the Republic of Venice – gave advice, which was not however followed. In 1541 and 1542, Michele Sanmicheli of Verona and Giulio Romano of Mantua were approached. We unfortunately know nothing of the nature of their suggestions, which were in any case not accepted.

This long planning history is surprising. On the one hand the approaching of so many respected architects underlines the importance attached to the project. On the other hand, there must have been unusual difficulties standing in the way of its realisation. These were probably of two kinds: firstly, previous conditions had to be considered in various ways, namely the existing main building of the Palazzo della Ragione dating from the fifteenth century and the fragments of the row of arcades that were begun by Antonio Rizzo in 1496 and continued by Giorgio Spavento in 1498, and which one evidently did not wish to fail to reutilize. Secondly, the completion of the loggias seems to have caused considerable static problems, as is indicated by the collapse of the first project.

On the basis of this past history and in the knowledge of the difficulties that the task would case, Giovanni da Pedemuro and his student Andrea Palladio developed an entirely new plan in 1546. This is the same point in time at which Palladio emerged from his commitment to the Pedemuro workshop. As he had been unusually thoroughly trained as a manual craftsman, the obstructions of the task seem positively to have lent wings to his imagination. At the same time the final shape of the loggias as described in detail above is certainly not the result of a spontaneous idea. A whole series of planning stages must have lain between the plan that he presented together with Giovanni da Pedemuro on 6th March 1546, and the final awarding of the contract to Palladio, which did not happen until 11th April 1549. Palladio will at the same time have once more thoroughly studied northern Italian architecture during these years.

Giulio Romano's garden façade for the Palazzo del Te outside the city gates of Mantua with its many serliana arrangements probably gave considerable impulses to Palladio's concept. More important is the fact that there was a model none too far away for this rebuilding of a representative town building with a two-storeyed loggia: the Palazzo della Ragione in Padua had been surrounded with two-storeyed arcades between 1420 and 1435. An arch arrangement in the lower storey is corresponded to here by two openings in the upper storey borne by slender marble supports. So there is a differentiation from top to bottom, the basement and main storeys are weighted differently. That Palladio had this Paduan building very clearly in mind during the course of his own considerations is proved by the fact that he takes over one motif: the oculi in the arch spandrels, which in Vicenza contribute so considerably to the spacious feeling of the wall, are borrowed from Padua.

A comparison with these stately buildings makes Palladio's distinctive achievement even more clear. The exceptional degree of unity appears in contrast to the Palazzo della Ragione in Padua, the heightened fusion of inside and outside in contrast to Giulio Romano, and the clarification of the architectural structure, by doing without the "picturesque" conception that is strongly characterized by decorative details, in contrast to Sansovino. That Palladio succeeds in creating an architecture extremely full of live despite what is first a positively rigorous standardization does not in the end make much difference to the importance of his creation. The slight irregularities of the dimensions of individual arcade arrangements are caused by the obligation to adopt already existing parts of the building – both vaulting and the re-casing of walled supports.

p. 73: Palladio's appointment as the chief architect of the basilica had been preceded by an extremely complicated construction history. The work on the core of the building was completed in 1458. The building of an arcade on the main façade was planned twenty years later, an untertaking which came to a standstill when those arch arrangements which had already been built collapsed in 1498.

Palazzo Iseppo Porto

Contrada Porti 21 (Vicenza)

With the exception of the Palazzo Antonini, Palladio built nearly all his palaces in Vicenza or, in a broader sense, on the Terraferma. While sketches exist which record his endeavours to build palaces in Venice, it was, however, not possible to carry out any of them. Yet his efforts failed less because of a shortage of clients than because of the pragmatic attitute towards life of the Venetian nobility. While merchants lived according to the rule of determing their expenditure by their income, the nobleman had to suit his expenditure to the requirements of his rank (Norbert Elias). As life in Italy, depending on the weather, was lived mainly in the open, this meant that rank had to be made most clear in the palace façade, without at the same time necessarily taking the ground-plan of the palace into consideration.

Vicenza was on the other hand, according to Norbert Huse, architecturally provincial at the beginning of the sixteenth century. Newly-built palaces did not, in contrast to Venice, have to compete in their architecture with already existing architectural traditions. In addition, Palladio there came into contact with a group of noble clients, who were, as he himself writes, willing to let themselves be persuaded by his ideas. That these expensive building plans often had to submit to practical considerations though, when this was made necessary by the client's financial state or his death, and that the carrying out of the original plan can most readily be determined on the façade, is another story.

One of these clients was Iseppo da Porto. Palladio designed a palace for him around 1549/1550, which was to have reached from the Contrada Porti to the parallel Via degli Stalli (the latter street name is more recent); but only the living block, which faces on to the Contrada Porti, was completed.

The lower part of the façade is rusticated. This might indicate a certain public function of the piantereno: as the owners' living quarters were usually situated in the piano nobile, the piantereno was used to accommodate the working rooms and the weapon stores. The fortress-like characteristics of the rustication would have also made this apparent visually. Palladio is not, however, content simply with rusticating the piantereno. The piantereno rests on a base which projects twice

"The following drawings show the house of Iseppo de'Porti, of the noble family of that name, in the town in question. The house faces onto two public thoroughfares, and so has two entrances each with four columns bearing vaulting and the area above. [. . .] The peristyle courtyard, which is reached down passages leading from the two entrance halls, will have columns thirty-six and a half feet high; in other words, as high as the ground and first floors taken together. Behind these columns are pilasters . . ., which bear the loggia above. The courtyard divides the house into two parts. The foremost is for the master of the house, and the ladies and maids. The rearward part is for guests, so that the hosts and guests do not need to take account of each other, something the Ancients (and especially the Greeks) paid particular attention to. In addition, the division will also be useful if the descendants of the nobleman I have referred to want their own separate living accommodation. I wanted the main staircase beneath the portico so that it would run to the heart of the courtyard and anyone who used it would as it were be obliged to see the most beautiful parts of the building, and also so that, being in the middle, it would be of equal convenience to both sides of the building." (Andrea Palladio, 1570)

and is smoothly plastered. The rustication over it is carried out in accordance with graphic models, and fits in with what is for Palladio a typical vertical structure. The windows are not merely cut out of the rustication: it is rather the rustication that supports their vertical characteristics: the window lintels form a trapeziform stonework cut straight across the bottom, which separates out into a star shape upwards and cuts into semi-circular blind arches. These blind arches are smoothly plastered and recessed into the surface of the wall. The blind arches themselves are shaped once again by a trapezoid stone work which projects above the blind arches, separating into the shape of a star, and whose keystone is decorated by a mask. This type of treatment of the façade, which is matched in the framework of the entrance portal, interrupts the monotonous square stone work of the piantereno and prepares us, both in the way it livens up our impression of the façade and emphasizes its vertical structure, for the richly decorated piano nobile.

For the first time on a palace façade, Palladio toys with the unbroken swelling movement of the half-columns in front of the wall. The columns are of the Ionic order, and correspondingly the entablature that they support is formed from a many-layered projecting ledge. The effect of moulded depth is heightened still further by the regular way it is offset above the column capitals. The profiles of the windows in the piano nobile protrude only weakly from the wall. The upper conclusions of the windows, on the other hand, are considerably more powerfully plastically shaped. They are characterized by a regular alternation of triangular and segmental arch gables that clearly project

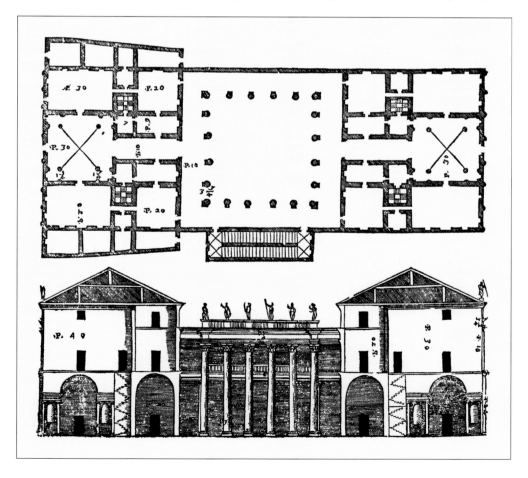

Right: ground-plan and elevation from the Quattro Libri. In this palace design, Palladio took his bearings from the houses of the ancients. Two residential parts were intended, one to be occupied by the master und mistress, the other to be at the disposal of guests of the house. Both compartments were meant to be connected by a courtyard surrounded by colossal column arrangements. Only a tiny part of the project was carried out.

in front of the wall. In the central and two outer vertical axes, the space between the window profiles and the columns is filled with ornamental garlands, which start at two sculptures resting on the gables. The plan published in the *Quattro Libri* intended such ornamental work for the entire width of the façade. As Ottavio Bertotti-Scamozzi saw and described its then condition as early as 1778, one can rightly doubt whether Palladio's planned ornamental work was indeed ever carried out.

The Palazzo Iseppo Porto makes rather a closed-off impression despite all the livening up of the façade. This is in no part caused by the rusticated piantereno; but even a piano nobile carried out in accordance with Palladio's ideas could not have effaced the impression that the wall is merely broken up by the added decorations, and not loosened up by any internal quality. Looking at the planned ground-plan, it seems in order to ask whether such a striving for openness could even have been reconciled with the ground-plan. As we have already seen, the Palazzo Iseppo Porto was intended to comprise two living blocks, which were to be separated by a peristyle courtyard with a colossal order of columns. The rooms of the noble owners would have been accommodated in that living block, which faces the Contrada Porti, while the guests of the house, in accordance with the model which Vitruvius recreated of Greek houses, would have been accommodated in the other living block. The owners' house was meant to be accentuated by two risalitos protruding at the sides of the building, whose rooms on the ground-plan do not have any organic connection with the room lay-out of the main part of the building. The atrium of the living block is reached through the entrance hall. From there one can reach the rooms which border it to the left and right. There is a clear systemization of the individual rooms to each other in this room lay-out. The size of the rooms is reduced continually, as later in the Palazzo Chiericati. The room lay-out of the Palazzo Chiericati is however dictated by the bordering walls, which surround the courtyard at right angles. In the Palazzo Iseppo Porto, on the other hand, the rooms are grouped at right angles around two small flights of steps. So in both living blocks two "snail rooms" (Herbert Pée) lie opposite each other, curling towards the outside. Thus the unity of the building seen from outside also has its equivalent in the ground-plan. With Palladio's tendency towards ground-plan arrangements with symmetrical axes, there is already a longitudinal axis in the Palazzo Iseppo Porto, which was meant to continue through the entire length of the palace. Even if its alignment is not disturbed by any penetrating cross-axis, we cannot yet speak of a subordination of the room lay-out to the domination of this axis; at this early stage it is rather the expression of Palladio's slavish orientation towards an organisation of the room lay-out with strictly symmetrical axes.

Above: not much of the ornamentation intended for the façade was carried out. Only three of the windows in the piano nobile are ornamented, with two sculptures on each. The areas between the window profiles and the columns are filled with stucco garlands.

Left side: the rusticated squares of the lower storey follow artistic examples which emphasize the vertical structure of the palace façade. In accordance with its function, the shaping of the piano nobile with its rich play of light and shadow in the rising and sinking forms is carried out in a somewhat richer fashion.

Palazzo Chiericati

Piazza Matteotti (Vicenza)

In the Palazzo Chiericati we encounter Andrea Palladio's only palace building to have been built almost completely according to his plans. On 19th May 1551 Girolamo Chiericati approached the Great Council of Vicenza to request permission for the construction work. In his petition – which was incidentally granted immediately – Chiericati says that the palace would be given a portico on the side facing the Piazza d'Isola for the decoration and improvement of the town of Vicenza.

If Chiericati was already able to make such a detailed statement about the project in the spring of 1551 – he himself says that he had consulted several (!) architects – we can assume that Palladio's plan can be dated as early as 1550. From 1551 onwards a lot of building was done on the Piazza d'Isola, which Chiericati kept a very thorough record of. The intention was evidently to bring the building project to a close as quickly as possible.

The southern part of the palace including the first intercolumnation of the loggia already stood in 1554. But the progress of the building work then slackened. This was probably caused by financial difficulties as well as the visitation of Vicenza by the Plague in 1556.

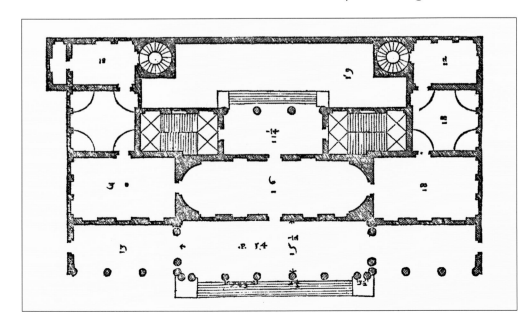

Left: ground-plan of the Palazzo Chiericati from the Quattro Libri. The vestibule that dominates the lay-out echoes the rectangular concept of the palace. The rooms that adjoin the vestibule to the left and right lie at right angles to the palace courtyard. Entrance to the courtyard is provided by a loggia, which is recessed between the two main flights of steps.

Girolamo Chiericati died in 1557; in that same year his son Valerio came into his inheritance. Substantial decorative work is recorded as having taken place inside the palace at this time. Apparently the part of the palace that had already been built was to be made as comfortable as possible in order, as has been verified by documents, to make it possible for Valerio Chiericati to move into the palace in 1570. In his will of 1579 he bequeathed four hundred ducats for the completion of the palace, but did not take much interest in the progress of the work. Stones were obtained with this bequeathed money; but the work on the single winged torso was not continued, so that Vicenza some years later felt obliged to require that the stones lying around on the Piazza Matteotti be cleared away.

Valerio Chiericati died in 1609. From this time onwards we no longer have any documentary evidence about the progress of the project. Not until 1746 is the building described by Francesco Muttoni as being completed. The town of Vicenza bought the Palazzo Chiericati in 1838 and started extensive renovation work. Since 1855 it has housed the "Museo Civico".

The ground-plan of the Palazzo Chiericati shows a lay-out which is laid around a courtyard at right angles in a strongly symmetrical fashion, and whose clearest characteristic is its transverse rectangular shape. One enters the palace through the portico in front of it and thereby reaches a transverse vestibule.

At this point the ground-plan of the piantereno is not identical with that of the piano nobile. The great sala in the piano nobile was an essential component of palace architecture. It was where the master of the house carried out his official duties and performed ceremonies. So one normally made every effort to make this room a sumptuous one. And this is just what Girolamo Chiericati did.

However idealistic Chiericati might have been in this respect, he was no different from other titled proprietors; a sala corresponding to the vestibule in the piantereno, which though wide was not very deep, would hardly have satisfied his ideas of a sala. While Palladio in his 1570 *Quattro Libri* portrays the Palazzo Chiericati as having a two-

pp. 80/81: the Palazzo Chiericati is situated on the Piazza Matteotti near the harbour. Its open architecture caused some researchers to assume that it embodied the type of the "villa maritima" – a villa near the sea. It possibly also represents part of a lay-out for the square, that Palladio intended to conceive along ancient Roman lines.

Right: elevation of the Palazzo Chiericati from the Quattro Libri. In this sketch Palladio presents the palace as "open" architecture. There is a two-storey column loggia in front of the main part of the building, which occupies the entire width of the rest of the façade. The middle section is offset slightly from the rest of the façade and is in addition emphasised by the massing of four close-together columns at its corners.

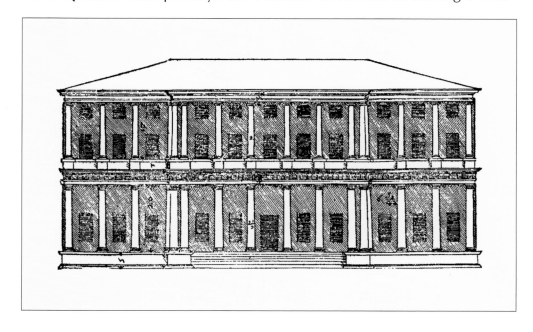

storeyed portico without a protruding central part to the piano nobile, this will most likely have been as a result of his own ideas.

But let us return to the ground-plan: the vestibule leads into the living quarters to the left and right, and through the entrance opposite one can reach the garden loggia, which is closed off by an arrangement of four columns and, flanked by two twin flights of steps, is recessed into the body of the building.

The plan intended there to be a wide flight of steps leading down to the courtyard, but this was not carried out. One of the first things to notice is that the size of the rooms decreases along the central axis up to the courtyard. This method of successive reduction in the size of the rooms is also taken up in the living quarters. The vestibule proves to be the most distinctive part, as far as spatial dynamics are concerned. The floor surface of the two rooms that border it on either end and of the rooms further back is steadily reduced.

How novel this was at that time is shown by one example of something that will also be of interest when looking at the façade of the Palazzo Chiericati. Let us consider Jacobo Sansovino's Villa Garzoni in Pontecasale di Candiana near Padua. Its ground-plan is also characterised by a symmetrical lay-out, which lies at right angles around three sides of a courtyard. The loggia on the garden façade, which is open in the piantereno, is continued in the upper storey in a closed form. From it, as if from a corridor, one can reach the various rooms of that wing of the building, which in the ground-plan all correspond with each other. So the principle which governs the ground-plan is – symptomatic of Renaissance architecture – an addition of rooms as in the Villa Garzoni as opposed to an opening out of rooms as in Andrea Palladio's first palaces.

In contrast to Palladio's other town palaces, the Palazzo Chiericati stands isolated on the Piazza and therefore dominates it, without being incorporated in a row of bordering houses. The decoration of the façade – we are talking about the portico – does, however, only characterize the side of the palace which faces the Piazza. While the Doric entablature is continued on the side wings, they are otherwise finished off smoothly and without decoration. So the question arises as to whether the Palazzo was indeed planned as the only building on the edge of the Piazza. So let us subject the palace façade to a close inspection: the first question that arises is whether the front side of the palace can at all be called a façade. It is characterized over its entire width by a two-storeyed portico. The sculptures set upon the upper concluding ledge must be ignored in this examination. They date from the seventeenth century, the time at which the palace was presumably completed. The sequence of the orders of the storeys is Doric for the piantereno and Ionic for the piano nobile. This order of storeys appears to be symptomatic of this phase in Andrea Palladio's work, as we can also find it at the Palazzo Antonini in Udine and the Villa Pisani in Montagnana.

As a protection against flood water and to make it possible to add cellars under the palace, Palladio had the palace built about five feet above ground level. A base entablature, on which the columns of the

"In Vicenza, on the square which is commonly called 'isola', Count Valerio Chiericati, a knight and nobleman of this town . . . has had a building erected. It has a protruding loggia as its lower part, which occupies the entire façade. The level of the ground storey is about five feet above ground. This was done both in order to accommodate cellars and other rooms there, which are useful to the house and which one would not have been able to put there had the cellar storey been entirely below ground, as the river is not very far away. And this was also done so that there would be a good view from the upper storeys."
(Andrea Palladio, 1570)

82

piantereno stand, reaches up to this height. The arrangement of the columns has a few peculiarities: all three entablatures on both sides of the palace are offset after the third space between the columns. At the point where the entablatures are offset, four columns are bunched close together, one of them following the pattern of the column arrangements of the wings, and a further one receding at an angle into the loggia. Two additional columns stand close together on the projecting entablature in front of the first column. This assembling of four columns close together forms a risalito, which in the piantereno corresponds to the width of the vestibule and in the piano nobile to that of the sala.

The internal arrangement of the palace is also recognisable on the front of the palace. Palladio justifies his use of four columns at the corners of the risalito in both storeys by referring to static necessity in

The palace differs from the published plan in the piano nobile. In order to get a room of a representative size, the client had the core of the building drawn up to the columns of the loggia for the width of this room. The rhythmic arrangement of the columns, and the windows and the rich ornamentation of the wall surfaces do however reduce the extent of this breach sharply.

Detail of the façade of the piano nobile. The windows of the piano nobile are crowned with a regular alternation of triangular and segmental arch gables, each of which is topped by two sculptures. In accordance with the order of the lower storey, the two floors of the palace are divided by a Doric frieze.

his *Quattro Libri*. But they doubtless also emphasise the central part of the palace to quite a considerable degree.

Palladio decorated the Doric entablature in correspondence with his ideas about the orders of storeys in the first of his four books about architecture: it consists of a regular sequence of triglyphs and metopes.

The piano nobile does not only differ from the piantereno in the changed order of the columns. The columns rest on pedestals, the spaces between which are closed by balusters across the entire width of the façade. The central part comes closest to what we consider a façade: here the sala is linked to the loggia and the core of the building is drawn out as far as the entablature. Consequently the columns do not appear plastically free, but incorporated into the stone work as half

A sculptural ornamental programme is set up on the roof of the Palazzo Chiericati, virtually as a continuation of the individual columns. The sketch in Palladio's architectural treatise did not intend such a programme. Indeed, in view of the overall impression of the palace, it has a disturbing effect.

columns. In each of the spaces between the columns there are a storey window and a mezzanine window that face onto the square.

In order not to endanger the incredibly intense play of light and dark through that part of the building that is drawn forward, strongly projecting triangular and segmental arch gables appear in a regular sequence between the ordinary windows and the mezzanine windows, each of them bearing two sculptures. The plastic window profiles also help break up the surface of the wall visually. So even the protruding loggia of the piano nobile can only slightly qualify the strong impression of the openness of the front of the palace.

So what is special about the front of this palace? What should first of all be realized is that an open loggia in the piantereno was certainly in keeping with the northern Italian building tradition. On the other hand, an opening in the piano nobile was not usual. At this point we can once again make a comparison with Sansovino's Villa Garzoni. It is not dissimilar to the Palazzo Chiericati externally. It is also arranged into a sequence of eleven vertical rhythms. Just like the Palazzo Chiericati, it too displays a change in the order of the storeys from Doric in the piantereno to Ionic in the piano nobile. Of the eleven vertical rhythms, here too five are on the central part of the façade and three on each of the outer wings. In the Villa Garzoni, which was built between 1547 and 1550, there is the precursor of one peculiarity of the Palazzo Chiericati, that is, the concluding of the storeys in a straight entablature. Sansovino attained the aesthetic basis for such a procedure, for he did not want to open up his loggias with columns, but with arch arrangements, and therefore applied half-columns onto the arch pillars, or pilasters on the outer pillars.

That such solutions were answers to what were certainly difficult

View through the open loggia of the lower storey. The coffered ceiling of the lower storey offers the same open impression as the palace façade. The individual panels are arranged with many layers.

problems for Renaissance architects is made evident by looking at the theoretical bases relating to this, which had been formulated both by Vitruvius and by Leon Battista Alberti: both speak of the impossibility of having an arch resting on a column. Only a straight entablature should be considered as a fitting conclusion to a column arrangement. Alberti even suggests that an arrangement of columns concluded by a straight entablature should be used in the porticos for the most distinguished citizens, whereas generally speaking an arch arrangement was suitable for town houses. So when Sansovino fuses the two, he is thereby ennobling his client. But in Palladio's case other considerations must have played a part. An arch arrangement in the piantereno would undoubtedly have militated appreciably against its impression of openness. Girolamo Chiericati certainly occupied a distinguished position in Vicenzan society and would therefore have been entitled to such an ennobling shaping of the façade.

But the portico, even though its central part is offset, still remains a curious thing which occupies the entire front of the palace. This oddity perhaps strikes us as less peculiar if we remember Chiericati's and Palladio's common interest in antiquity. Old wall paintings occasionally depict villas near a harbour that have a two-storeyed open portico. As the Palazzo Chiericati was situated near the harbour, it was occasionally associated with such a villa marittima. What argues against this is the way the portico is connected to the palace façade: it is placed in front of the palace like an additional room layer, without being dynamically linked to it. We must exclude the protruding sala from our considerations, as it can be traced back to the client and does not stem from Palladio's own plan. An open portico which is placed in front of the façade as a screen leads us perforce to assume that the façade has less the function of being an external status symbol of the palace than of presenting itself as a component of the square, namely the Piazza Matteotti. First clues in confirmation of this assumption are given by Girolamo Chiericati's petition of 1551 to the Great Council of Vicenza, in which, as has been discussed above, the façade facing the square was given special reference as an adornment to the town of Vicenza.

Palladio's own ideas, which theoretically were probably completely in keeping with those of his client, substantiate and reinforce this assumption. In the third of his four books about architecture, he described the Roman square lay-out. In this description, if all four sides of the square are to be built around, he expressly requires that an open two-storeyed loggia should be added in front of the buildings. For the lower storey would serve as a protection against the weather, whether it was raining or sunny, while the upper storey would have the function of affording a good view. The drawing that was produced with this description makes a comparison with the Palazzo Chiericati as a possible component in such a plan to seem thoroughly justified.

This appears even more plausible if we turn back to the description of the Palazzo Chiericati in the third chapter of the second book of the *Quattro Libri*. The raising of the building by five feet above ground level was, apart from its practical function, also meant to afford a pleasant view. All this confirms the supposition that the Palazzo Chiericati could have been a first step in the shaping of the Piazza Matteotti in the style of a Roman square. Consequently its portico would not have been a function of the palace, but of the square.

"The Romans and Italians, who, as Vitruvius wrote, departed from Greek custom, made their squares longer and wider, so that, if the length was divided into three parts, two parts would be equal to the width. Because they presented the gladiators with gifts on these squares, this form seemed more suitable to them than the square shape, and for the same reason they built the porticos, which encircled the entire square, to have spaces between the columns that were two and a quarter or even three times the diameter of the columns, so that the people's view would not be hindered by the thickness of the columns. The porticos were as wide as the columns were long, and there were shops and stalls in the areas below. The columns above were a quarter smaller than those underneath, as the lower constructions had, with regard to the weight they had to carry, to be stronger than the upper ones, as I have already said in my first book."
(Andrea Palladio, 1570)

Villa Cornaro

Piombino Dese (Treviso)

The Villa Cornaro is an example of a type of villa which Andrea Palladio also built, at almost exactly the same time, for Francesco Pisani in Montagnana. This villa has a complicated building history. It was commissioned by Giorgio Cornaro, descendant of one of the protagonists of the villegiatura, Alvise Cornaro. The central part of the building must already have been built by 1553.

In 1554 the work on the Villa Cornaro was discontinued. But just as little of the side wings of the villa had been built as had of the column arrangement of the upper loggia. Even though further construction work was done on the villa in 1567, in 1582, on the occasion of the registering of the inherited estate, Marco and Girolamo Cornaro, the sons of the now deceased Giorgio Cornaro, emphasized that the inherited house had not been completed yet. All the same the upper loggia was finished in 1596. Whether at this point the side wings had also been completed cannot be definitely established.

At any rate Girolamo Cornaro provided in his will of 1655 that a considerable sum of money should be used to continue building the villa. This testamentary provision did not furthermore only cover the construction work; the continuation of the internal decoration was included in it. The construction history of the villa is just as complicated as its position in Palladio's work is interesting.

His early villas were characterized by a width-orientated ground-plan. This meant a clear separation of the living and representational areas for the impression of the room lay-out to be apparent on the outside of the villa. The living quarters were at the side of a central compartment, whose representational function was revealed by a correspondingly altered façade decoration or even by arch arrangements. Even though the central compartments were given a separate treatment, the bordering compartments existed with almost the same rights next to them, and this all the more, as the formal vocabulary that was used – arch arrangements, risalitos or rustication – was no doubt intended for the remaining façade compartments, but was not organically connected with them to form an indivisible whole.

For the first time in the Villa Poiana, Palladio's will to fuse the living and representational areas of a villa harmonically with each other is

"The following building belongs to Mr. Giorgio Cornaro of Piombino in Castel Franco. The main hall is in the inmost part of the building, where it is equally protected against heat and cold. [. . .] There are mezzanine floors above the small rooms. The upper loggias are of the Corinthian order, and smaller by a fifth than those below them. The rooms have flat ceilings and there are mezzanines above them. The kitchen and storage rooms are on one side and the servants' quarters on the other." (Andrea Palladio, 1570)

expressed. The Villa Cornaro represents a clear continuation of this endeavour. In contrast with earlier villa buildings, the mansion stands on an almost square ground-plan. The great room is the dominating part of the room lay-out. Its emphasized position within the arrangement of the rooms is naturally also caused by its size; but what is also important is that the development of the sequence of rooms is subordinated to it. In accordance with the body of the building, this room is characterized by a square ground-plan. By dint of its size it forms a link between the portico and the garden loggia which is recessed in the building. The garden loggia is flanked by two flights of steps, as is the case in the Villa Pisani in Montagnana. The volume of the rooms increases steadily starting there. In connection with this, the fact that the side wings are incorporated harmonically in the arrangement of the rooms is remarkable. Their width is identical to the width of the two

Right: ground-plan and elevation of the Villa Cornaro from the Quattro Libri. The ground-plan shows a systematic fusion of the room layout of this mansion and side wings into an harmonic whole. The four-columned main room occupies a dominant position. It combines the spatial forces of the room arrangement in itself.

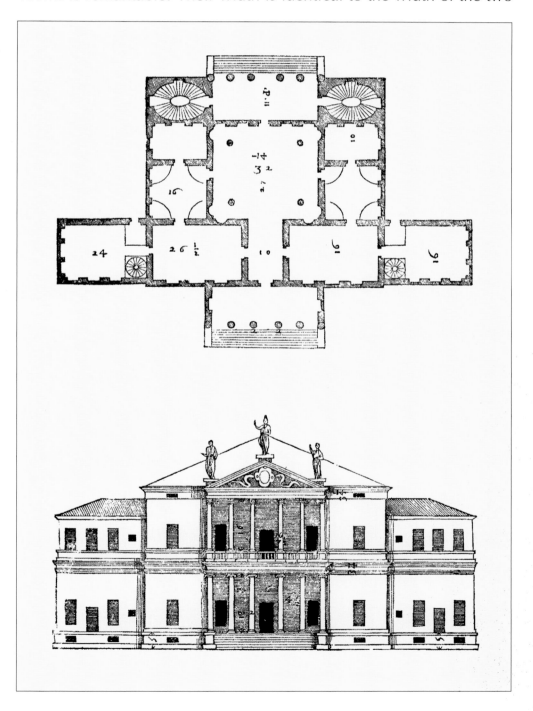

pp. 90/91: view of the garden of the Villa Cornaro. We know that even in 1553, Giorgio Cornaro and his spouse often spent time at this estate in Piombino Dese for "relaxation and practical reasons". At this point, however, the construction work on the villa was still in full swing.

The loggia, which is recessed into the core of the building on the garden side, clearly protrudes from it on the main façade. Its width corresponds to that of the four-columned room inside the building.

rooms on either side of the entrance hall. This organic fusion of the living quarters with the working area is new; equally new is the central position of the great room. The façade of the Villa Cornaro also tells of the stylistic innovations on the inside of the villa.

One thing must however be considered when examining the Villa Cornaro and its façade, and that is the fact that, if one judges from an aesthetic point of view, it cannot really be measured against the type of the villa rustica. Evidently Palladio, when designing the villa, let himself be guided primarily by an aesthetic point of view and subordinated the conception of functional buildings to the stately character of the lay-out. The Villa Cornaro differs further from the type of the villa rustica, whose main characteristic can be seen as a one-storeyed layout, in the doubling of the piano nobile, and thereby comes close to

Although the Villa Cornaro is situated near a stream, its main façade faces the street that runs past it. A wide outside staircase leads up to the front loggia. The loggia's columns are Ionic.

being a villa suburbana, a country seat outside the gates of a city. This typological relationship is also expressed in another respect: although a small river flows past its side, the main façade faces onto the street that runs along past the villa. In addition, the bordering buildings come up relatively close to the Villa Cornaro, so that it is robbed of the possibility of dominating a large area. If one looks at all this together, it proves to be stylistically close to the Villa Pisani in Montagnana and the Palazzo Antonini in Udine (which may be either palace or villa – it is difficult to say). The doubling of the piano nobile corresponds to a positioning of two loggias, one above the other. Both the garden loggia and the loggia on the main façade are carried by free-standing columns. On the garden façade the loggias that are recessed into the building make it possible for the columns to be free-standing; on the

main façade on the other hand, they stand in front of the building like a portico. The internal arrangement of the villa can also be read on its outer shape. This is not in contradiction to the statement that the two rooms of the side wings correspond in their width to the two bordering ones of the mansion house; the solution to the problem is original: the stonework of the main façade is stronger than that of the side wings.

The organic fusion of the working and living areas is also taken into account on the façade. The Ionic entablature of the lower storey order lies like a belt around both the side wings and the mansion house. Nonetheless the subordinated position of the side wings is not ignored visually. The doubling of the storeys is interrupted at the side wings. In place of a second storey two mezzanine storeys appear there, which noticeably fall short of the height of the second main storey of the mansion house. But even in the shaping of the front of the mansion house priorities are established which make clear the connection with the ground-plan of the villa. The width of the loggias corresponds to the length of the sides of the great room. But this is not the only way the motifs correspond. Next to the correspondence of the measurements there appears the requirement that the representative character of this quasi-public part of the building be expressed. We have already discussed the square ground-plan of the villa. But the gable too is of compellingly stately character. It is drawn down to the height of the

Above: the construction work on the Villa Cornaro dragged on for several generations. Instructions in wills ensured the continuation of the work, which must have been a great burden to each heir.

Above: "Columns should be present in an even number on the façade of a building, so that there is an intercolumniation in the centre. This should be made a little larger than the rest, so that one can see the doors and entrances all the better, which should normally be put in the middle of the building."
(Andrea Palladio, 1570)

p. 96: the Cornaros were one of Venice's old noble families. They clearly indicated the way they saw themselves in the so-called four-column room of their villa in Piombino Dese. Sculptures that portray prominent members of the Cornaro family were put up in the six wall niches. The artist was Camillo Mariani.

p. 97: while the Villa Cornaro must have been ready around 1655, the work on the inner decoration continued. Bartolomeo Cabianca carried out various pieces of stucco-work as late as 1716.

Corinthian entablature and gives the appearance of being carried by the columns of the loggia. It evidently does not serve as the crowning of the house, but rather as the crowning of the stately area of the villa. The dwelling apartments, on the other hand, close with the surrounding Corinthian entablature. All of these formal references to the hierarchical structure within an organically self-contained whole are heightened once more by the way the bordered walls are staggered back. This staggering starts at the loggia. The layer of the wall which next lies behind it marks the living area, to which the side wings are subordinated by receding once more.

From all this it becomes clear that the formal vocabulary no longer functions as a decorative means of conveying a message, but appears as the external sign of an internal arrangement.

Villa Pisani

Porta Padova (Montagnana)

The Villa Pisani lies outside the Porta Padova of the town of Montagnana, only four kilometres away from the Villa Poiana.

Montagnana was fortified in the fourteenth century by Francesco da Carrara, but fell to the supremacy of Venice in 1405. Two mills were situated outside the town; they had been built by Carrara and were driven by a stream, the Fiumicello. The Venetian nobleman Francesco Pisani had his villa built by Andrea Palladio over this narrow watercourse during the 1550's. The villa is the very model of the type of the villa suburbana and from the start housed a workshop. The new building is mentioned in documents for the first time in the year 1553. At this time the Villa Pisani must for the most part have been completed. The construction work appears to have been essentially finished by 1555.

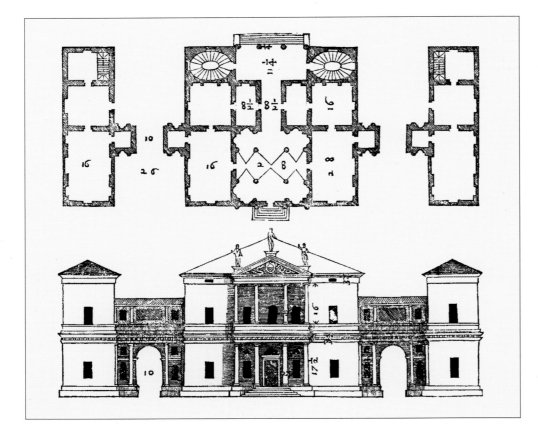

Left: ground-plan and elevation of the Villa Pisani in Montagnana from the Quattro Libri. The Villa Pisani lies directly next to one of the town gates of Montagna. The sketch that was published in the Quattro Libri planned that this "villa suburbana" should be annexed to the walls. There is however no evidence that this intention was ever translated into action. Only the mansion figured in the plan was built.

p. 99: garden façade of the Villa Pisani. From the start, a workshop was fitted out in the Villa Pisani. Francesco Pisani had his Montagnana villa built over the Fiumicello, a stream which also fed the mills which dated back to the time of the Carraras.

Both the doubling of the piano nobile and the massive unity of the street façade allude to motifs from palace architecture. Contemporaries must have had similar feelings. In documents which concern this villa, it is usually referred to as Francesco Pisani's "palace".

A palace belonging to Francesco Pisani is often mentioned in documents. The functional character of the Villa Pisani can on the other hand not be denied, and the reference at the beginning to the mills that Carrara built was not made by chance: the Pisani family held the rights to these mills, whose running will have brought them considerable profit. That the Villa Pisani was not a building with an agricultural function is shown by the lack of agricultural buildings on the estate. Francesco Pisani was a town Venetian and his villa therefore had to fulfil representative functions.

Palladio's *Quattro Libri*, which has already elsewhere been found guilty of inaccuracies, speaks of an estate which had an arched building added to left and right. One of the two extensions was intended to reach over the town moat with its arch and, it if had been built, would have connected with the town walls of Montagnana. We can no longer ascertain today whether the lack of these extensions is to be explained by Pisani's death. Probably the drawing in the *Quattro Libri* can once again be attributed to Palladio's endeavours to present ideal architecture in his treatise. The building as it was carried out must therefore be seen as having been planned in this shape for Pisani.

The street and garden façades of the Villa Pisani are shaped differently. This is of interest in our examination, as it helps us most clearly understand the combination of villa and palace architecture in the villa suburbana. The street façade presents itself as being closed, almost like a fortress. As in his town palaces, Palladio again tries to wrest a certain dynamism in the play of light and shadow from the closed wall surface; so the peace of the strongly geometric proportions of the windows meets the swelling movement which the four columns produce. The triglyphal frieze which runs around the building bows to this interest in a modelling of the façade. The Doric order of the lower storey, simple in itself, is decorated by Palladio with a regular alternation of bucraniums, round discs and triglyphs. As Erik Forssmann remarks, the equal status of both storeys can be read in the use of different storey orders.

The gable, with its opulent decorative modelling, also contributes to the impression of tranquillity. The situation is different on the garden façade. That which is linked in with the body of the building as half columns on the street side here appears plastically free, which is made possible by the two-storeyed loggia, which is recessed into the body of the building, so that the latter stands on an almost square ground-plan. Here too the windows are geometrically proportional, without however making a strict impression. On both façades the central part is slightly offset from the façade. On the garden façade, this supports the subordinating character of the loggia, which subjugates the flat façade compartments to its dominance. So the garden façade can be understood as an answer, suggesting openness, to the closedness of the street façade.

In the piano nobile, four Ionic columns bear a mighty gable, which is richly decorated with stucco-work. The coat of arms of the Pisani family is emblazoned in this gable area. Beneath the gable, an inscription identifies Francesco Pisani as the person who commissioned the building.

Villa Chiericati

Vancimuglio (Vicenza)

The attribution of this villa to Palladio cannot be advocated with absolute certainty. We lack documents which name the architect. Above all, however, Palladio did not mention the building in his *Quattro Libri*.

The villa is mentioned for the first time as a work by Palladio by Muttoni in 1740. Beyond this, some signs of his authorship can be offered. The drawing of a ground-plan by Palladio that is kept in London is very similar to the building as it stands. And its commissioner, Giovanni Chiericati, was the brother of Girolamo, for whom Palladio had designed the Palazzo Chiericati in Vicenza.

We are better informed about the date of its building than about who designed it. On 29th April 1557 Giovanni Chiericati asked his heirs in his will to complete the building which he had started in Vancimuglio. Presumably the villa was largely finished at that time, and the plans were probably made sometime between 1550 and 1554.

The stylistic appearance of the building is decisive in attributing it to Palladio, and here elements that are closely related to Palladio mix

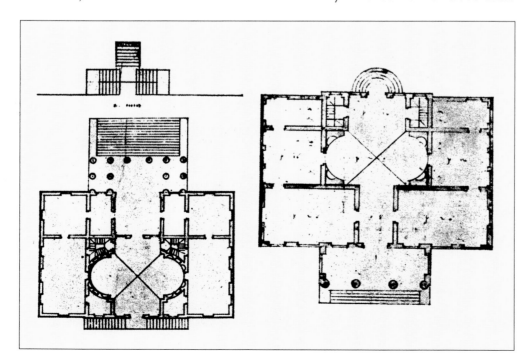

The Villa Chiericati is not identified as one of Palladio's works in his architectural treatise. Palladio was mentioned in connection with the villa in 1740 by Francesco Muttoni. This drawing, which is by Palladio, is kept along with ground-plan sketches (RIBA XVI, 20) which suggest such a connection at the Royal Institute of British Architects in London.

Right: Giovanni, brother of Girolamo Chiericati, who had the palace on the Piazza Matteotti in Vicenza built, commissioned the Villa Chiericati.

pp. 104/105: Palladio incorporated a colossal column order in a villa for the first time here in the Villa Chiericati. The portico that is formed by this column arrangement is positioned in front of the main part of the building. The windows of the side rooms on the main façade which press outwards are however rather unusual for this phase in Palladio's creative work.

Below: detail of the sculptural programme. Giovanni Chiericati, who commissioned the building, was obviously very interested in the building scheme being completed with regard to the decorative fittings also. In his will, he asks his heirs to continue the started construction "(with) all the appropriate and necessary remaining parts."

with conspicuous differences from the villas he was working on at that time: in front of the cuboid self-contained main building, the columns which project on one side only form their own square, whose bordering side walls are more strongly closed off than, say, those in Piombino Dese. The colossal order in place of the two storeys could be pointing ahead to the villas Malcontenta and La Rotonda.

While on the one hand the façade is strongly concentrated towards the centre, the window axes which are moved a long way out cause what are more like centripetal accents on the side wall surfaces – a preliminary stage in just such a tense relationship as will in a very different shape characterize the Villa Rotonda.

Not least, the fact that unusually large and unshaped wall surfaces remain between the rectangular and mezzanine windows is conspicuous: there are closed walls just where one normally expects the piano nobile. Not least, the arrangement of the flanks into a structure with a regular beat – four window axes, thus no emphasis of the centre – is unusual for Palladio.

Palazzo Antonini
Via Palladio (Udine)

There are no great problems involved in attributing the Palazzo Antonini to Andrea Palladio. Our architect describes this palace, which "Floriano Antonini, a nobleman of this town (Udine) has built from the ground upwards", in the second of his four books about architecture.

In his description of the palace, an otherwise taciturn Palladio goes into detail concerning some of this building's peculiarities. He first of all mentions that the first storey – meaning the ground floor – was carried out in rustication. This is in itself not exceptional, and even Palladio's own work includes some buildings, whose basement storeys were carried out in a rustication. It is however remarkable that Palladio did not hesitate to rusticate the half-columns of the front façade, of all things, while, with exception of the windows, which are set in small rusticated stone squares, the façade itself was smoothly plastered. The architect, who was otherwise more likely to abide by those rules which Vitruvius set up for architecture, here appears – just as he does a good ten years later at the Villa Sarego in Santa Sofia – to fall back on a rather more modern motif, that Michele Sanmicheli in particular often used in Verona. The Palazzo Bernardini in Lucca also has rusticated columns. Such a rusticated column goes against classical principles, as a column should never give the impression that one could take it apart into its constituent pieces, as this would visually militate against its supporting character. Nonetheless, the columns of the lower storey bear witness to a certain mightiness, for they reach beyond a likewise rusticated straight entablature, which serves as the upper conclusion of the windows.

Another peculiarity noticeable in the lower storey of the front façade is the five mezzanine windows, which lie over the four windows in the spaces between the columns and the entrance portal. This arrangement corresponds with the intercolumniation of the piano nobile, but is not continued on the rest of the façade. While the arrangement of the mezzanine windows in the loggia-like central part of the façade matches the drawing that Palladio published in his *Quattro Libri*, this same drawing of the Palazzo Antonini also shows a lower storey, in which the stone work of the intercolumniation is rusticated, but not the actual columns. It is possible that the rustication of the columns can be

"Now we however come to those buildings, of which the following is situated in Udine, the capital of the Friaul, and was built from the ground up by Floriano Antonini, a nobleman of this city. The first storey of the façade has a rusticated order, and the columns of the entrance façade and the lower loggia are of the Ionic order... The kitchen lies outside the house, but is nonetheless set in a useful position. The privies are next to the stairs, and even though they are placed within the body of the building, they produce no unpleasant smell whatsoever, as they are installed in places that are far away from the sun, and as some air shafts lead from below through the wall up to the top of the roof."
(Andrea Palladio, 1570)

attributed to a wish of the client. But the possibility should not be ignored that Palladio himself, when he published his treatise on architecture, considered the rustication of the columns to be no longer justifiable and simply published the drawing of the plan in a modified form.

Interestingly enough, Palladio only uses this motif on the front façade. The garden façade, which along with the sala in he piano nobile reminds one of the Palazzo Chiericati, has smoothly plastered columns placed one on top of the other, Ionic in the lower storey and Corinthian in he piano nobile. As with so many of his buildings, here too one should not overlook the fact that the Palazzo Antonini could not be completed in Palladio's lifetime. Assuming that the construction work started in 1556, the work very soon came to a standstill. Evidently only the two front loggias can be brought into accord with

Right: ground-plan and elevation of the Palazzo Antonini in Udine from the Quattro Libri. The ground-plan of the Palazzo Antonini shows some similarities with that of the Villa Pisani in Montagnana. The view of the façade also shows forms which are similar to the shaping of the façade of the Villa Pisani.

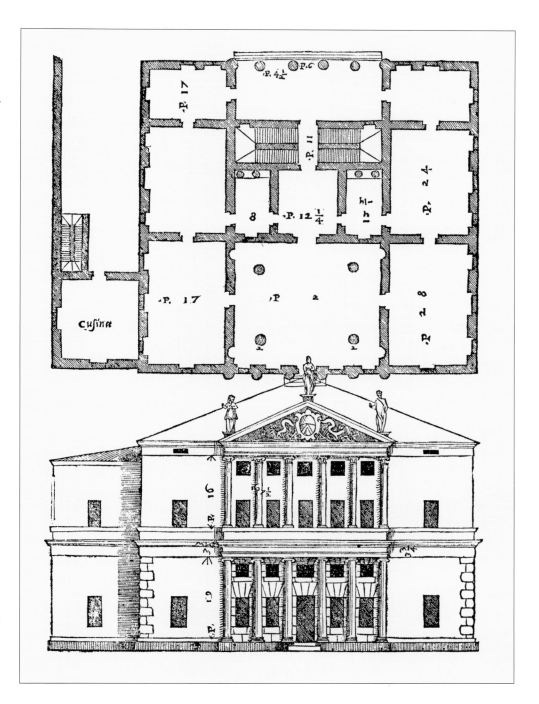

pp. 108/109: although the Palazzo Antonini is situated right in the centre of the town of Udine in the Friaul, Palladio used elements of villa architecture in his concept. This led to this town palace occasionally being called a "villa suburbana".

107

IL PICCOLO

PALAZZO ANTONINI
ora sede della Banca d'Italia
Progetto di A. Palladio
1556
Affreschi di M. Fischer 1769
e di O. Politi 1825

Above left and right: contrary to the drawing in his architectural treatise, Palladio had the wall surfaces of the Palazzo Antonini smoothly plastered. Instead, both the columns of the lower storey and the window frames were carried out in a rough rustication.

Palladio's sketch, even though the planned gable over the loggias was not carried out. Inside the building only the atrium appears to be in agreement with Palladio's plan.

The rest of the building, which today houses a bank, was completed in later years; the internal decoration was done in the eighteenth century by the painter Martin Fischer.

According to the plan, there were plans for a wing bordering the main building to the left. This wing, which was never built, leads us back to Palladio's description of the palace in his *Quattro Libri*. His conviction, recorded in another part of this architectural treatise, that the quality of a building can be measured by its convenience and its utility as well as by its durability and beauty, led him in the case of the Palazzo Antonini to solutions which he obviously held to be successful enough to be worth mentioning. He mentions the kitchen and the toilets. The kitchen was meant to be incorporated in that wing, which was not built. And "although it is outside the house, it is nonetheless situated appropriately". His incorporation of the "privy", as he calls it, is interesting if only because waterclosets were not around yet in 1556. Therefore he needs some justification for placing it within the body of the building. For "they produce no unpleasant smell whatsoever, as they are installed in places that are far away from the sun (Palladio chose small rooms next to the stairs) and as some air shafts lead from below through the wall up to the top of the roof."

p. 110: "The order of the first floor of the façade is rustic, the columns of the entrance façade and the lower loggia are Ionic." (Andrea Palladio, 1570)

111

Villa Badoer

Fratta Polesine (Rovigo)

If one considers the Villa Cornaro in Piombino Dese, which was designed four years previously, the Villa Badoer seems almost to be a retrograde step. The emphasis on the large hall as the main part of the building which draws the spatial forces onto itself, now comes second to the earlier formal principle of a row of three longitudinal axes. Also, the villa is no longer characterized by the distinctive stately character of the Villa Cornaro. Nonetheless, its design cannot be seen as a retrograde step. With regard to the villas he built, Palladio's work is in the end characterized by his not having developed a single type of villa, but rather by his having applied the aesthetic convictions that he gained from his building experience to the individual type of build-

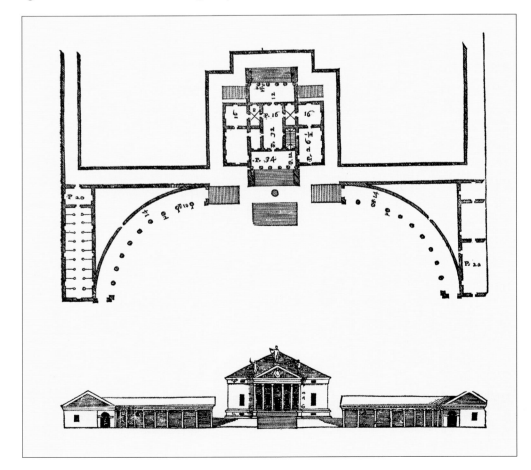

Ground-plan and elevation of the Villa Badoer from the Quattro Libri. The quadrant of the "barchesses", which are set up in front of the farm wings, are an unusual feature for Palladio's work. The farming wings were extended in the eighteenth century. It is possible that the "barchesses" were not included in these extensions for financial reasons.

In this picture, a wrought-iron portal lets us through to the villa. The interested visitor is however advised to find out about the opening hours of the villa, which is owned by the state. Because these are constantly changing and anything but regular, it is not unlikely one would fail to find the entrance portal of the Villa Badoer so invitingly open.

pp. 114/115: the Villa Badoer is one of those villas which were built as the visible sign of a completed process of cultivation. It was raised above ground level in order to protect it from flood water from the nearby river. That its do-minant position within the estate was em-phasized by this is something that will surely have fitted in well with the ideas of the client.

ings. In this respect the paramount difference between the villas Cor-naro and Badoer is of a practical nature.

With its single-storey lay-out and its long barchesses, the Villa Badoer proves itself to be an agricultural functional building. Fran-cesco Badoer, who commissioned Andrea Palladio to build the villa in the vicinity of the village of Fratta in the Venetian Polesine, was a Venetian nobleman. At the beginning of the sixteenth century, the Polesine was a broad plain, in which the waters of the Adige and Po rivers rose and formed side branches which turned usable arable land into a swamp. In the course of measures introduced by Alvise Cornaro, the Polesine was included in the "Retratto di Lozzo" and the arable land was reclaimed it by bit from the swamp. Like many Venetians, Francesco Badoer saw agriculture to be an equally profitable and safe investment. The estates in the Polesine which belonged to him had previously been inherited by his wife.

The villa, which has come down to us in exceptionally good condi-tion, must have been built around 1556. Only the farm buildings differ from their original state. They were extended in the eighteenth century and brought up to the front walls of the estate. Previously they had ended at the barchesses. The whole lay-out of the villa stands out due to its remarkably homogeneous unity. Whenever the barchesses, which opened towards the front, are described in literature about

Venetian villas, a comparison with human arms is attempted. Indeed their positioning at right angles with the mansion house gives them the force to direct our eyes. This fits in smoothly with the ideology of villa culture, which wanted to have all the forces of agricultural work centred on and increased in the mansion house of a villa's complex. The comparison with human arms appears to be especially valid in the case of the Villa Badoer. Of course, as with many other villas, the farm buildings also are at a right angle to the mansion, but the latter is outplayed by the quadrant of the barchesses, whose movement inevitably arrests the eye of the visitor and forces it along to the mansion, which is raised above ground-level.

In order to bridge the difference in height between the farm buildings and the mansion, there is a many-sectioned flight of steps leading up to the front loggia. In contrast to the Villa Cornaro, the front loggia here is not an external symbol of a part of the internal arrangement of the villa. So the crowning gable is not meant to be understood as a representational sign of the public part of the villa, but rather as the representative conclusion to the entire mansion. This exceedingly harmonious unity of the lay-out is not disturbed by any sort of decoration. Its simple formal vocabulary fits in smoothly with the complete homogenous organism of the villa and as a result mediates harmoniously between the aesthetic and representative requirements of the villa lay-out.

117

Villa Barbaro

Maser (Treviso)

The phenomenon of the country residence (villegiatura) is not one that would have arisen all at once and without any preparation. It has its origins in various areas, all of which are connected with the history of Venice at the beginning of the sixteenth century. Venice's wealth came from its overseas trade, whether as the result of the sale of imported goods, or of the processing of the imported goods for the Venetian luxury market; and one can safely say that, around 1500, the majority of the Venetian population was directly or indirectly connected with the sea trade. This went so far that even grain had to be imported; the fact that on the Terraferma outside the gates or the city fertile fields were turning into swamps appears not to have bothered anyone at the time.

If, however, a crisis were to develop in this all-important sea-trade, what would be the effect on a city with such a one-sided economic structure? In 1453, the signs of just such a crisis began to appear with the loss of Constantinople to the Turks, which was the beginning of an increasing expulsion of the Venetians from their trade centres in the Eastern Mediterranean by the Turks. The Venetian trade crisis began to take on threatening proportions, however, when in 1497–98 the Portuguese Vasco da Gama found a direct sea route to India. This caused the Venetian caravan routes to lose nearly all their significance. That alone already meant a marked economic loss for Venice; when the League of Cambrai then moved against Venice and involved the Republic in armed conflict, Venice's financial sources threatened to dry up due to the high cost of war.

The financial losses which had arisen in Venice did not constitute the only problem, which confronted the Serenissima after the conflicts; the one-sided reliance of Venice on sea-trade meant that, should it become endangered, a sharp rise in the numbers of unemployed would be the inevitable result. Indeed this problem must have taken on quite considerable proportions in Venice. A third factor arose: the fact that Venice was dependent upon imports for its supply of grain led increasingly to severe difficulties in its providing supplies to the populace. The cause was a constant alternation between shortages of money and inflation, the extent of which was given by a contemporary source in the admittedly lengthy period of time between 1400 and 1580 as being 50 percent of the value of gold. Even the opening up of new trade routes to north and eastern Europe could not counteract this development.

In 1523, Andrea Gritti entered upon his term of office as Doge. The situation, as he saw it at the beginning of that term, was more than merely serious. On the one hand he wanted to do everything that was within his power to make future difficulties in the provision of grain impossible. That his gaze, in the course of these endeavours, should fall upon the Terraferma, was quite unterstandable. On the other hand, the estates there had in many cases been neglected. Of the 800,000 fields on the Terraferma, 200,000 were no longer of agricultural use.

A thorough reorganisation of the public administration of the Terraferma now took place. In the course of these measures, the first step was the severing of Venetia from the Habsburg fiefdom, which resulted in the Doge of Venice becoming at the same time the duke of the surrounding mainland provinces. The next step was to start drain-

Right: ground-plan and elevation of the Villa Barbaro from the Quattro Libri. Like the Villa Rotonda, the Villa Barbaro was built for a client educated in humanism, who possessed the financial means for the realization of an ideal type of building. Unlike the Villa Rotonda, the Villa Barbaro was not emulated in later villa culture.

pp. 120/121: Palladio chose a colossal column order for the façade of the mansion of the Villa Barbaro. The forms of the Villa Barbaro go well with each other due to their simplicity and balance. They form an harmonic unity with the surrounding landscape.

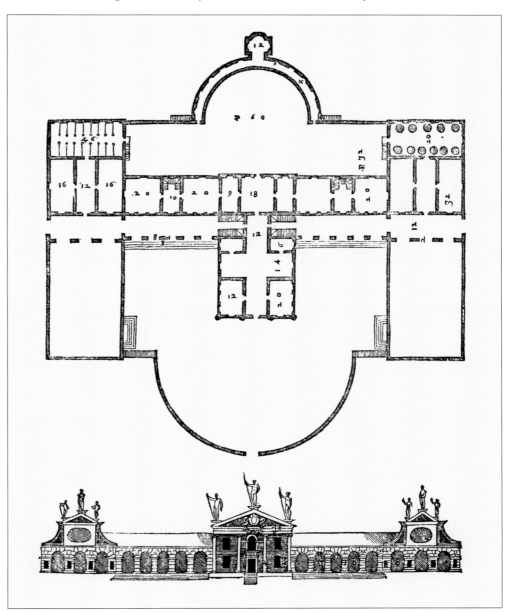

Leonardo once wrote: "Where there is beauty, there cannot be any usefulness." While this opinion of Leonardo's may be contradicted in many Venetian villas, it is true in the case of the Villa Barbaro, that, despite its relationship with villas that were erected principally as functional buildings, it mainly provided for the relaxation and humanist studies of its owner.

ing the marshes. The Venetians had a centuries-old tradition where water was concerned. The need in the following period was to create an irrigation and drainage system on the Terraferma that would assist both the areas with little and with rather too much water. The discovery of such a system can be traced back to the Arabs. The increased use of this system in Italy originated in Lombardy, and Venice indeed made use of engineers from Lombardy to turn their plan into action.

If the external circumstances which can count as one reason for the country residence are now clear, one must nevertheless not overlook the fact that these alone are not sufficient to explain the phenomenon of the country residence. For in those areas in which from 1540 onwards an abrupt increase in the number of planned villas is to be noted, fields were at that time already being cultivated. But all at once a change took place in the way the Venetian nobility thought. The concept of agriculture was placed on a metaphysical level. The spokesman for this development was Alvise Cornaro. His family belonged to the old Venetian nobility and was closely connected with Venetian trading companies. In the general crisis, however, the busi-

Above: the mansion protrudes a good way in front of the arcades. Through the deliberate differentiation in the structure of the façade, of the middle compartment from the neighbouring façade compartments, Palladio is revealing a representational area inside the villa. The shape of the middle window of the piano nobile is worth a comment. Its concluding round arch is decorated with luxuriant fruit branches and breaks into the lower ledge of the gable.

pp. 124/125: "The level of the upper rooms is equal to that of the rear courtyard, where a fountain built into the hillside opposite the house lies, decorated with countless stucco ornaments and paintings." (Andrea Palladio, 1570). The possibility of having their villa built near a spring was extremely important for the humanistically educated Barbaro brothers. An iconographic programme which included the entire arrangement of the villa could be developed from its symbolic meaning.

ness enterprises of the Cornaro family collapsed. Alvise Cornaro came to the conclusion that any economic future would have to be appreciably oriented towards agriculture, and took the appropriate steps. He had settled in the vicinity of Padua, and within a short period of time he had managed to enlarge his estate greatly and to profit considerably from it. He had come to recognise the connection between water technology and the cultivation of land an early stage. Venice's orientation toward agriculture, which continued to increase after 1530, can be seen as his achievement. As a sign of his commitment, the "Magistratura sopra i beni incolti", which was an authority for unexploited lands, came into being in 1556.

His success should however not be ascribed only to the practical advantages of agriculture, which Cornaro was able to make clear to the Venetian noblemen by the example of his own success in agriculture. Having himself been influenced by a humanist education, he well unterstood the humanist ideals that could be seen in agriculture. With Varro, Cato and Columnella, ancient literature was able to offer the works of authors who had formulated the ideals of agricultural

In his monograph on Palladio, Lionello Puppi compares the façade of the Villa Barbaro with a sketch Palladio did of the Temple of Fortuna Virilis. There are indeed striking resemblances, suggesting a sacred interpretation of the Villa Barbaro need not be altogether ruled out.

management. In the opinion of Alvise Cornaro, agriculture suddenly took on a sacral character. In his writings he constantly refers to it as "santa agricoltora" – "holy agriculture". In his treatise *Discorsi intorno alla vita sobria – Discourses on a temperate life* – this sense of mission takes on a clear form.

His very words are, "I can therefore rightfully assert, that I have raised an altar and a temple to the Lord my God and have presented him with souls, that pray to him." The concept of the villa came to fruition in the so-called "villa books", which were widely circulated in the sixteenth century. At first sight we may see in that a reaction to the time of crisis, which in compensation for reality sought flight into a firmly-based peaceful ideal. We should however not overlook the necessity in Venice of relocating the excess that the economic crisis had caused. In fact the renewed agricultural activity after 1540 was supported to a high degree by the town-dwelling Venetians. The Venetian government supported would-be settlers by making necessary equipment and experts available. Moreover, credit as well as tax relief was granted. But in the main it was the Venetian nobility which settled on the Terraferma.

The conjunction of practical necessity and the idealisation of a life on the land as a result of humanist thinking was the precondition for the appearance of the country residence, although two differing tendencies in the building of villas came into being. Depending on the priorities which were set by the noble clients, there either arose villas which had predominately the characteristics of an estate, or those which as country residences sought to convert into concrete form the spiritual ideals of villa life as the creation of an "Arcadia", of a charming place untouched by reality.

The giant among these villas is the one that Andrea Palladio built at Maser, near Treviso, for the brothers Marcantonio and Daniele Barbaro. One can without any reservations whatsoever describe it as the most complete villa creation of Palladio's. In contrast to his brother Marcantonio, who played a leading role in the administrative affairs of Venice, Daniele Barbaro was a member of the clergy and, as the Patriarch of Aquileia, took part in the Council of Trent. He made no secret of his humanist ambitions, and the association between these two spiritual directions was quite natural to him. Sources assure us quite believably that Daniele, who was closely befriended with the protagonist of the country resience, Alvise Cornaro, sometimes gave his humanist interests precedence over his spiritual duties.

There are many indications that the Villa Barbaro must have been built around 1557–58. It could not have been more fortunately situated: the villa complex includes a spring, which was situated half-way up a gently sloping hill. There were at the time all sorts of conjectures connected with this spring, which amounted to the fact that there must in earlier times have been a place of worship there, possibly even a temple. Marcantonio Barbaro designed a nymphaeum for the spring, which was meant to accentuate its symbolic content as a mediator between the heavenly and earthly elements and give the place a sacred character, as it were.

View through an arbour at the side of the Villa Barbaro. The villa's arbours are closed off by arch arrangements. If one ignores their rhythmical qualities, then arcades are part of a simple formal language. By dressing the arcades with smooth stones, they have become an harmonic whole with the façade of the mansion.

Let us turn first of all to the front façade of the Villa Barbaro. Palladio had always arranged the façades of his buildings in pronounced vertical planes. This principle is taken to even further lengths on the façade of the Villa Barbaro. The alternation of segmental arch gables and triangular gables does not here occur in the horizontal, but in the vertical axis. The triangular gables crown the windows of the upper storey, and the segmental arch gables those of the lower storey. The farming wings are flanked by two columbaries. Two quadrant arches lead down from each crowning gable in a smooth descent to the level of the single-storey farming wing. We should notice, incidentally, that a slightly protruding building comparment is formed by this process which singles out a three-arch arrangement within the farming wings on both sides.

127

Sun dials decorated with astrological symbols have been incorporated into the square panels on each blind arch. In this process we can see the endeavour to give the Villa Barbaro a sacred splendour, for the importance of astrology for the Renaissance and its church architecture should not be underestimated. In connection with the Villa Barbaro, it is of some interest to us that a member of the family, Ermolao Barbaro, came to the public's notice with an astrological treatise concerning the influence of the heavenly bodies upon human life.

This display of astrological interest is however not the only clue that makes the endeavour to give the villa a sacred splendour, which can probably be attributed to Daniele Barbaro, comprehensible. There is the crowning of the façade by a gable connected with four Ionic columns, which is a motif that has been transferred from ancient temple architecture to secular buildings. For all that, the crowning of a façade by a gable is not at all uncommon. In the sixteenth chapter of the second of his four books about architecture, Palladio himself writes that in all his villas, and also in some of his town houses, he put the gable on the front façade, where the main doorway was, so that this gable could indicate the entrance to the house, and promote the greatness and glory of the work by raising the front part of the building over the remaining parts. Nonetheless, the gable on the front façade goes beyond its duty to the stately image of the building. Palladio himself gives a hint to such a further interpretation in his description of the villa in his *Quattro Libri*: "The façade of the mansion has four columns of the Ionic order, and the capitals of the side columns are shaped on two of their sides. I will describe in my book about temples how these capitals are to be made."

If we include this observation in our examination, then Lionello Puppi's conjecture, which connects the façade of the Villa Barbaro with the plan of a façade for the Temple of Fortuna Virilis, which Palladio had reproduced in the thirteenth chapter of his fourth book about architecture, gains a high degree of probability. Nonetheless, the main building does not derive its dominant function solely from the motifs borrowed from sacred buildings. The spectator's eye is drawn to this part of the estate by the rhythmic balance of the circular shapes, which begins in the columbaries and is greatest in the middle of the mansion's façade. In addition, the mansion protrudes a long way in front of the farming wings.

It seems fair to ask whether this fusion of sacred and secular elements has any equivalent within the villa. The plan of the villa gives us no direct information about this, even though the base of the main room is characterized by a cruciform shape. The frescoes are of importance in this context. Paolo Veronese's signature shows him to be responsible for them, just as he is for the decoration of the grotto behind the nymphaeum. It is here at the very latest that the endeavours of the clients to have an idealised illusory world built within the real world become apparent. In the paintings, motifs from everyday life are connected with ones of a sacred nature. Paolo Veronese's ability to

The stucco work in the gable of the Villa Barbaro is attributed to Allessandro Vittoria. In his description of ancient villas, Palladio gives his reasons for having used an entrance gable as, amongst other things, its suitability "for affixing the symbol, that is, the coat of arms of the builder". Here in Maser the Barbaro family's coat of arms is surrounded with rich stucco work.

create illusionistic paintings peaked at the Villa Barbaro. What is illusion and what is reality? one is often tempted to ask. Windows framed by columns afford a view of Arcadian landscapes, whose idealised character is underlined by the appearance in them of ancient ruins. Right next to them there are real windows, which make it possible to see the real landscape. The resulting interplay is impressive: is the real landscape ennobled by this new connection with the idealised landscape, or is the claim to reality of the painted landscape heightened and manifested by being next to the real landscape?

This question seems difficult to answer. Nonetheless, the illusory paintings extend over all areas of the villa's inner decoration. A painted halberd stands in one corner, and out of an illusory door there steps a painted hunter, returning home from the hunt with his dogs. What is interesting is that in the main room of the villa, the Hall of Olympus, we move from a secular realm to a sacred realm. On a surrounding balustrade we see various people who are dressed according to their era, are pictured in lifesize, and appear to be watching the goings-on in the villa. The iconographic programme of the main room reaches its zenith in the vault fresco over this balustrade. We are dealing with a representation of Olympus, in the centre of which there is the allegory of wisdom, surrounded by the gods of the firmament and their attributes. These sacred representations can all be found in the storey from which one can reach the nymphaeum and its spring.

If we take all this into consideration, then the Villa Barbaro can indeed be seen as a building whose lay-out was conceived with the aim of linking the secular with the sacred. If at first it is the secular aspect that predominates, we then find in the Hall of Olympus a reconciliation of both aspects, a kind of preparation for the estate's "Holy of Holies", the spring. Through the fact of its having as it were been built into the hillside, the Villa Barbaro becomes an attribute of the spring with a character that prepares us for it.

Beyond this, Palladio's endeavour to connect architecture and landscape harmoniously with each other attains a heightened expression through this device, which in the Villa Barbaro creates an ideal work which has remained unparalleled in all villa building.

p. 131: the frescoes in the cruciform room of the piano nobile are with respect to their themes closely connected to villa life. In this process, the illusory painting provides an impressive alternating play of appearance and reality.

pp. 132/133: Paolo Veronese is the master who carried out the fresco decorations in the rooms of the villa's piano nobile. Views through actual windows are contrasted with such painted on windows, which lead into landscapes with ruins from antiquity. As an expression of the harmony of villa life, musicians appear in painted niches holding in their hands instruments such as the hurdy-gurdy, which were, during the Baroque, still regarded as typical pastoral instruments.

Villa Foscari

Malcontenta di Mira (Venice)

On the banks of the Brenta lies one of Andrea Palladio's most beautiful villas. Its main façade, with an imposing free-standing column portico, faces the canal. Standing on a mighty base, if offers the visitor approaching the villa by water a sight of impressive majesty. The villa lies close to the gates of Venice. It is named after its owners, Nicolo and Alvise Foscari. But it is known under the name which it borrowed from the little town to which it belongs: Malcontenta. In order to have the main façade facing the river, Palladio broke with tradition and built it facing north instead of south. "It is a fine and wonderful thing, if one can build a villa by a river, as produce can at any time be conveyed at little cost by boat to the city. In addition, the river would be very useful both for domestic purposes and for the animals..." Thus wrote Andrea Palladio on the occasion of his deliberations on the most favourable situation of a villa.

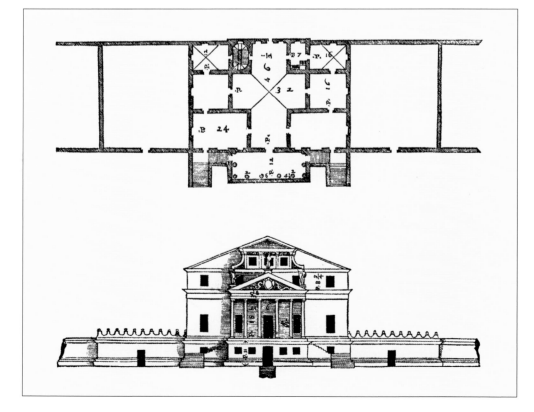

Villa Foscari, called "La Malcontenta". Ground-plan and elevation from the Quattro Libri. The Malcontenta was planned as a country residence. Information about it can be gained not least from the drawing of the plan, which did not provide for farming wings. These wings were added in the seventeenth century, but have been completely destroyed in the mean time.

The aspect of utility can easily be neglected with regard to the Malcontenta. Nicolo and Alvise Foscari had their villa built as a country residence between 1559 and 1560. It completely lacks the farm buildings that are a necessary part of a villa. In fact, a complex of farm buildings was added to the Malcontenta in the seventeenth century, but they no longer exist today. So the villa is once again present in the form in which it was conceived.

One is tempted without any intention of irony to use the term "villa temple", which Alvise Zorzi coined for Palladio's villas. Indeed it seems, like the Villa Barbaro in Maser, to have been developed partly from a religious theme, and that not only with regard to the motif of the gabled column portico which was borrowed from ancient temple architecture. Humanist thinkers were thoroughly familiar with the connection between ancient and Christian religious beliefs; the Christian religion was seen as the heir of the ancient religions, and so the constant appearance of ancient forms in no way contradicts thoughts concerning the use of a religious scheme.

Palladio's clients were nearly all moulded by humanism. Gutenberg's invention of the printing process was enthusiastically received in Venice, and simplified access to the authors of antiquity made it possible to presuppose a knowledge of these authors among a large proportion of the nobility. Palladio's own commitment to antiquity has already been mentioned repeatedly. Of his drawings of ancient buildings, one is of special interest to us, the one which is kept in the Museo Civico in Vicenza and represents the temple over the spring of Clitumnus. The importance of the spring has already been discussed in the chapter on the Villa Barbaro in Maser, and its symbolic content was firmly rooted in the connection between the worldly and heavenly elements of humanistic thinking, especially with regard to the ideals of

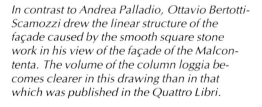

In contrast to Andrea Palladio, Ottavio Bertotti-Scamozzi drew the linear structure of the façade caused by the smooth square stone work in his view of the façade of the Malcontenta. The volume of the column loggia becomes clearer in this drawing than in that which was published in the Quattro Libri.

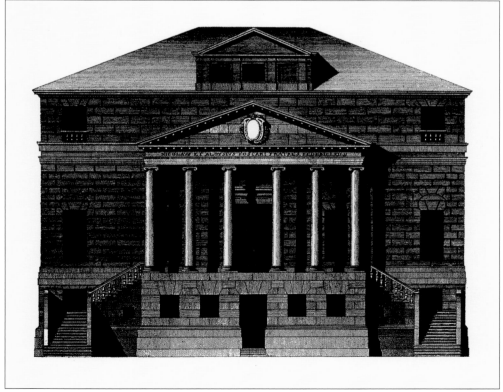

the "vita in villa". In Maser the spring was included in the overall scheme of the villa by use of the nymphaeum. The Malcontenta lacks any such spring that could be included in the villa programme. Nevertheless, formal references seem to have been given, which in the sense of an "architecture parlante" seek also to include this aspect of the ideal villa in his conception of this villa.

If we turn to the above-mentioned drawing of Palladio's, we can establish that the temple that he portrays stands on a huge solid base broken in the centre by a portal. A portico rises above it, which is crowned by a gable bordered by consoles. These motifs appear once again in modified form on the façade of the Malcontenta that faces the water-course, both on the greatly elevated base and on the column portico and the console-bordered gables. Such an "architecture parlante" does not seem unlikely, if one additionally considers the fact that the façade on which this motif is used is situated directly by a watercourse. Palladio's ambitions as regards the water have already been pointed out. Of course, it is not meant to be a case of pointing to a spring that actually exists, but rather one of taking a villa ideal into account through a formal reference.

When one enters the villa by the portal, one finds oneself abruptly in the main room of the building. The aligning of the main room according to a cruciform ground-plan can be unterstood as a resumption of the principle, realized in the Villa Cornaro, of the centralising of all the building's spatial forces on one main room.

Palladio's attitude towards mathematical harmony is once again made clear in the arrangement of the rooms around this main room: the development of the rooms is accomplished by a continual increase in the volume of the rooms by taking the size of the preceding and following rooms as a basis for this. The cruciform shape is masked by this grouping of rooms, expanded into a rectangle and is no longer noticeable on the façade.

So the main room of the piano nobile acquires its dominance not through its correspondence with the exterior form of the Malcontenta, which seems to derive from a square-shaped block, but rather through its inherent centripetal forces is able to subordinate all the other spatial forces of the interior arrangement.

Because the Malcontenta faces north, the main room is lit from the brightest or, in other words, the southern side. Palladio used this fact to his advantage. The side opposite the entrance is transformed into a veritable wall of light. A large thermal window takes on the shape of the room's vaulting. Underneath it, there are three further windows, which fit into an illusory painted architecture and reduce the wall, which is normally experienced as a limitation, to a minimum. This wall of light ensures that the room is properly flooded with light and thus supports the concentration of the spatial forces on its centre.

Because one comes abruptly into this room straight from the entrance, it has a public function. Its decorative work is correspondingly rich. In accordance with the ideals of villa culture, the subject matter of the paintings is themes from ancient mythology, surrounded by a painted sham architecture. At this point we are once again made

Villa Foscari. Detail of an engraving by Giovanni Francesco Costa (?–1773). Comparison with Palladio's own drawing of the temple at the spring of Clitumnus (detail below) shows striking similarities. The resemblance suggests there might be some justice in a symbolic view of the Malcontenta's main façade.

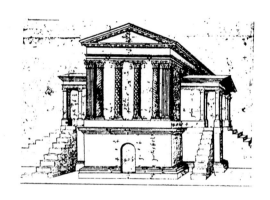

p. 136: "It is a very fine and pleasant thing to be able to build a villa by a river . . ." (Andrea Palladio, 1570). The Malcontenta lies on the Brenta canal immediately outside the gates of Venice. The main façade, which was supposed to face the water, was built facing north, contrary to tradition.

Above: the forms of the Malcontenta are systematically related to each other or link up with each other. Thus, for instance, the round-arched thermal window which cuts into the gable of the risalito, a trick which underlines the rising tendency of the risalito and sets it off from the remaining part of the façade.

p. 138: light is an essential aid to the shaping of the garden façade of the Malcontenta, which is built facing south. Contrary to the main façade, the centre part is offset only slightly from the façade. In the place of a plastic modelling, Palladio preferred a linear structuring produced by rusticated squares in this the Malcontenta's garden façade.

aware of the fusion of the inside and outside of the building into a harmonic whole. The sham architecture created by the painting is of the Ionic order, as is the storey order of the piano nobile on the main façade.

How, then, is this fusion expressed on the façades? Let us begin with the main façade. Its outward appearance is determined by the portico, which takes into account the size and position of the base and extends backwards by three intercolumniations. The width of the loggia indicates the entire width of the central room. There are colour-contrasted ledges on the façade, which is rusticated in a moderate fashion, and these form a clear division of the piano nobile from both the ground floor and the mezzanine storey. The Ionic columns with their capitals scrolled down at the sides support this tendency of division. The column order of the portico stretches from the base in front of the main part of the building up to the ledge, which closes off the piano nobile at the top. The function of the loggia as the border of the subordinate compartments of the building, at the same time displaying the dignified character of that room whose representation it undertakes, can be seen even more clearly here on the main façade of the Malcontenta than at the Villa Cornaro. The strengthening of the subordination of the bordered compartments through their additional recession into the wall is also indicated at the Malcontenta: because of the considerable

degree to which the piano nobile's ledge projects, the mezzanine gives us the impression that it is receding.

The same principle of subordination, albeit achieved by other means, characterizes the garden façade. Here also the colour-contrasting ledges mark out the extent of the piano nobile, and a part of the façade, which is equivalent to the width of the loggia, crams up against the surface of the wall and thereby exposes the great room of the piano nobile. The gable of the main façade is replaced by a broken gable, which connects harmoniously with the rising form of the thermal window.

Above: "In all my villas, and in some town houses, I have mounted the gable onto the front façade, where the main doors are, so that these gables may indicate the entrances of the house and serve the greatness and splendour of the work by raising the front part of a building above the remaining parts."
(Andrea Palladio, 1570)

p. 141: the architectural order of the main façade is also taken on by the paintings in the cruciform room. The columns of the painted architecture are of the Ionic order. Allegorical figures are framed by these columns.

pp. 142/143: view to the side of the cruciform room which is opposite the windows.

p. 144: Battista Franco was active as a painter in the Malcontenta alongside Giambattista Zelotti. Franco died in 1561 and left the fresco in the Hall of the Giants unfinished.

p. 145: the dull colours of the frescoes are a sign of the threat that increasing air pollution poses to works of art.

Santa Maria della Carità

Accademia di Belli Arti (Venice)

The reconstruction of the Convento della Carità was Palladio's first extensive commission in Venice. The convent was owned by Lateran canons, and since about 1500 they had been intending to have it completely renovated. They had an ambitious systematization of the badly arranged older remaining buildings in mind. On 7th March 1561 the name of Palladio, who at that time made a model for the work on the convent building, appears for the first time in the documents. So we can estimate the beginning of his work on the design at about 1560.

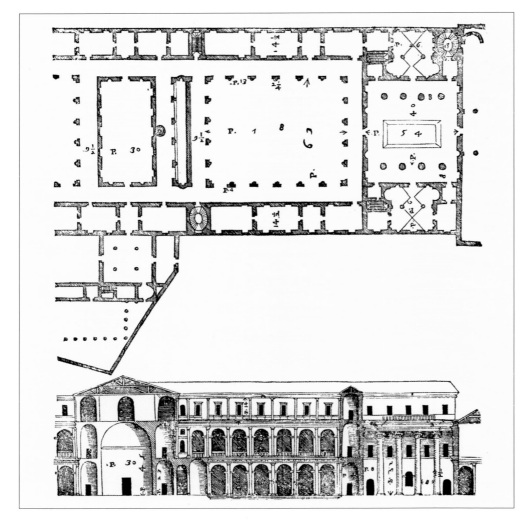

Ground-plan and elevation of Santa Maria della Carità in Venice from the Quattro Libri. According to his own statement, Palladio wanted to bring this building into line with ancient houses. Economic problems, however, led to the extensive project being only partly completed. This fragment was badly damaged by a fire in 1630.

Right: two arcade storeys of equal dimensions are followed by a low storey. This arrangement of the view of the courtyard is based on ancient theatre buildings rather than on preconditions of an ancient peristyle courtyard.

"Above all I hurried to the Carità: I had found in Palladio's writings, that he had here dealt with a convent building, in which he intended to represent the private houses of the rich and hospitable ancients. The plan, which had been drawn admirably both as a whole and in its individual details, gave me great pleasure, and I hoped to find a veritable marvel; but alas! hardly a tenth of it was completed; but even this part is worthy of his heavenly genius, having a completeness in its lay-out and an exactness in its execution, which I had not previously seen . . . Dear Fate, you who have favoured and immortalized many a foolish thing, why could you not let this one work be achieved!" (Johann Wolfgang von Goethe, 2ⁿᵈ October 1786, Venice)

On 1ˢᵗ June 1561 he is named as the "director" of the work, and on 14ᵗʰ May of the following year he received twelve months' pay. In the following period his presence at the building site can no longer be proved.

Economic difficulties and obviously also the moral decay of the convent meant the extensive project was only partially completed, and moreover, the fragment was heavily damaged by a devastating fire in 1630. All that remained was a wing of the cloisters, which Goethe admired, along with the sacristy and a spiral staircase. A ground-plan and a sketch in Palladio's *Quattro Libri* give us an approximate idea of the original plan, even though we must assume that the author here produced an altered draft of his original concept.

According to Palladio's own words, in the Convento della Carità he wanted to reproduce an ancient Roman house on a monumental scale. In his drawings, an atrium with colossal rows of columns at the sides marks the beginning of the entire lay-out. It is flanked symmetrically by the sacristy and chapter-house. There follow the rectangular three-storeyed cloisters, to which the other convent buildings are joined. Nevertheless, the reference to the example of a Roman house should only be unterstood in the most general sense.

It has been pointed out with some justification that the design of the cloisters, the fragment of which is nowadays included in the Galleria delle belle arti, points stylistically to Palladio's classical phase rather than to his later period, in which he was committed to dynamic tendencies.

147

San Giorgio Maggiore

Isola di San Giorgio (Venice)

In 982 the island on the southern side of the basin of San Marco was given by the Republic of Venice to the Benedictines. In the following centuries, the convent gained an extraordinary importance in economic affairs and church politics, which from the fifteenth century onwards made an extensive renovation of the convent and church possible.

After Palladio had already built the refectory between 1560–62, he was in 1565 commissioned to design a new church. Palladio had

San Giorgio Maggiore. Longitudinal section according to Ottavio Bertotti-Scamozzi. Because the thermal windows in the side aisles correspond to the semi-circle of the arcades, each of the individual bays is experienced, as one walks forward, as a transverse axis entire in itself. The motif of the thermal windows is taken up again in the upper floor of the main room.

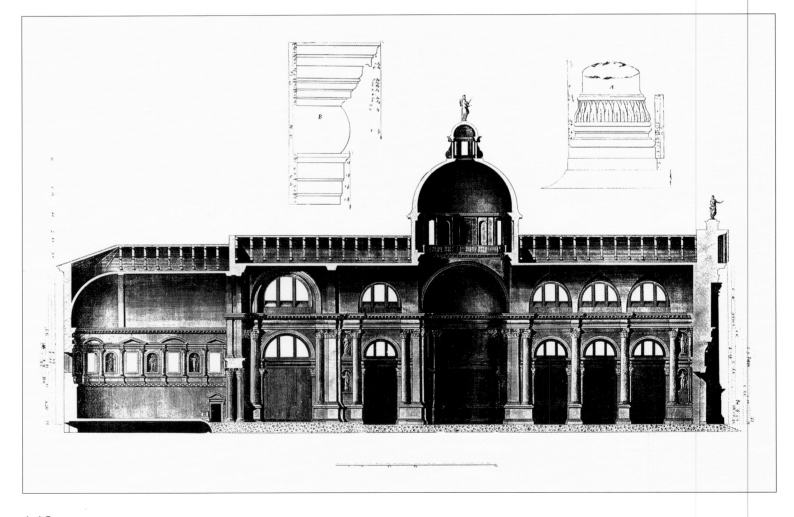

produced a wooden model, and the laying of the foundation stone followed in 1566. He held the post of building director until 1568, but his design seems to have been carried out conscientiously in the following period. In 1575 the enclosing walls of the church area and the drum over the crossways were already in position, the dome was built one year later, and in 1591 the long monks' choir was completed. The final part of the work was the erection of the façade during the years between 1597 and 1610.

In the townscape of Venice, San Giorgio Maggiore is of decided importance. The church and convent are a visual complement to the buildings on St. Mark's Square. No other architect of his time was destined, like Palladio, to fulfil the conditions of such an angle of view, for he had previously included landscape perspectives in an idealised form in several of his villas.

Compared to the façade of San Francesco della Vigna in Venice, built later, Palladio differentiates the relief of the wall structure in favour of a dynamic intensification towards the centre. The side axes which correspond to the side aisles are framed by pilasters, which are doubled at the outer corners. Gravestones in column tabernacles on high pedestals are placed in front of the surfaces of the walls. Palladio adopted a local tradition of Venetian church building of the Renaissance in doing this. At the same time, these monuments, from a formal point of view, indicate the connection and combination of the flanks

San Giorgio Maggiore. Ground-plan according to Ottavio Bertotti-Scamozzi. The main building has the appearance of a rectangle and qualifies the impression of a cruciform basilica, which clearly predominates in the external view, with a long transept.

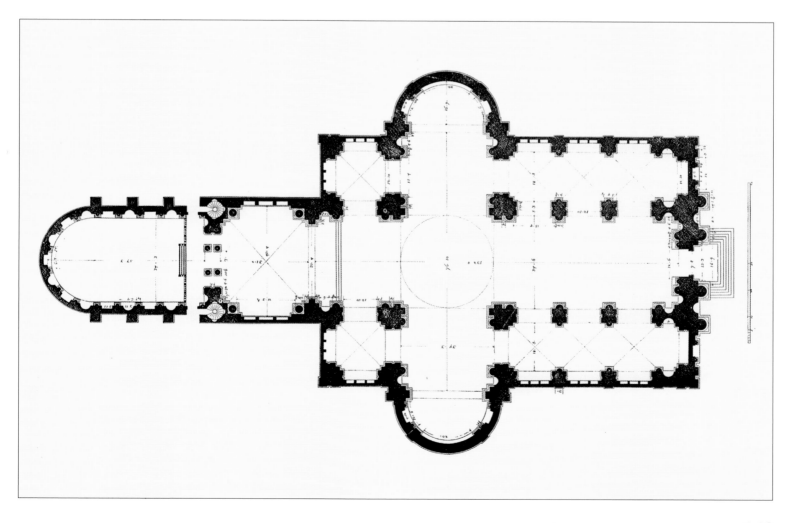

and the dominating central block: they first of all introduce on a small scale the motif of the columns, then determine, by the height of their bases, the high pedestals of the colossal columns, and also prepare us for the motif of the triangular gables.

The part of the façade in front of the main aisle creates the impression of an open temple portico, behind which a solid wall extends. Next to it the central column arrangement, which once again serves the "crescendo" from outside to inside, is considerably widened in contrast to the side intercolumniations. Three-quarters of the bodies of all four columns protrude from the wall and thereby strengthen the impression that they are free-standing. Weaknesses in this concept appear when seen close up, as Jacob Burckhardt recognised.

There is hardly any cause to doubt the authenticity of the façade design, nor to consider the possibility of later alterations: such details diminish in importance in favour of the overall appearance when the decisive long-distance effect towards the Piazzetta of San Marco is taken into account. Especially impressive is the way the view of the façade unfolds when viewed close up from the waters of the Bacino di San Marco: the "temple gable" is lower than the dome, the accord of white ashlar, red brick and white roofs is experienced in full harmony, and the dominating vertical line of the central part of the façade balances the far-projecting arms of the transept that emphasize the horizontal line. The campanile was added in the eighteenth century, as a counterpart to the great campanile of St. Mark's, one further element that connects the Piazzetta of San Marco with the complex of buildings on the Isola di San Giorgio.

The ground-plan and sketch of the inside, which in each case were developed according to strictly worked-out measurements, differ in an extraordinary manner. The definite prevailing impression of the external aspect of a cruciform basilica with a long transept is seen in relative terms in the ground-plan. The main building appears as a rectangle with conches added on at the sides of the crossways. Its length corresponds exactly to the length of the transverse axis. The side aisles, which are half the width of the main aisle, continue on the other side of the transept with one further bay, which is built over a square ground-plan. An unusually long monks' choir that ends in a semi-circle follows on from the square presbytery.

Upon entering, the first impression is one of a decidedly longitudinal building with an exceptionally clear structure and great dignity. The three bays of the nave are split up by colossal columns of the Corinthian order that stand on high pedestals. They possess composite capitals, that is to say, that fusion of Corinthian and Ionic capitals which was developed in Imperial Roman times, was used throughout the Middle Ages and once again became the predominant capital shape during the Renaissance. A rich and distinctive entablature, which receives its featherlike elegance from a broad swelling, is offset above them. Here Palladio developed further a motif, which he had already used on the basilica in Vicenza. A powerfully modelled console ledge projects over it. Due to their very nature, these offset parts demand to be continued in the vaulting. This is done only partially, in

p. 150: the heightening of the values of expression on the façade of San Giorgio Maggiore clearly increases towards its centre. This can in part be attributed to the widening of the centre intercolumniation of the temple front, that lies before it. The supports, which become a dominating element of the façade structure by their plastic expression caused by the change from weakly protruding pilasters to colossal three-quarter columns, play a decisive rôle in connection with this.

that the sharply-cut groins of the lunettes start above the projecting top of the entablature. They connect the round arches of the three-part thermal windows with the barrel vaulting, which embraces all three bays, and which was evidently never intended to be decorated.

By means of the arcades, the side aisles are both separated from and connected to the main area. Double pilasters with Corinthian capitals are placed in the arcades, and are closed off by an entablature which is closely related to the upper conclusion of the colossal order in the main aisle, and once again emphasises a convex curved link. The double order of these pilasters widens the arcade arrangements to narrow arcade walls, which close the side aisles off relatively emphatically from the main area. On the other hand, the juxtaposition of the pilasters directs one's gaze to left and right, along the side aisles.

The structure of the side aisles is very similar to that of the main area. Half-columns on both sides bear an offset ledge which is profiled in the same manner; the outer walls recede into niches on a rectangular ground-plan, so that here too the half-columns receive pilasters on their reverse sides. In each bay, a gabled tabernacle altar is set up on the outside wall. The thermal windows above the entablature correspond to the half-circle of the arcades, so that as one walks forwards one is always in a transverse axis entire of itself. At the same time, these

Above: Composite capitals were used throughout the Middle Ages and once again became the predominant form of capital during the Renaissance. Palladio uses them both on the inside and outside of the church of San Giorgio Maggiore. "The composite order which is also called the Latin order, because it was invented by the Romans, is called composite, because it shares in both the above orders (Corinthian/ Ionic) . . . The composite capital has the same measurements as the Corinthian one. It does however differ from it in the volutes, the eyes, the semi-circular moulding and the ovolo moulding . . ."
(Andrea Palladio, 1570)

thermal windows connect the cross-vaulted bays of the side aisles with the structure of the main area.

The overall view from the entrance to the choir is richly rhythmical, both with regard to the structure of the walls and the vaulting. The strongly accentuated pillars of the crossways – pilasters ordered at right angles to each other and flanked by three-quarter columns – bear the dome above round arches that open equally to all sides. Pedentives – sail-shaped curved triangles – connect the square ground-plan of the crossing and the circular beginning of the tambour, the dome storey, which behind a balustrade is arranged alternately with niches and window openings. As light also enters through the crowning lantern, the area of the crossways appears as the centre of the building, linking the horizontal line of the nave with a vertical line of vision. Because the balustrade has the effect of blurring the beginning of the tambour, the dome appears to be floating.

The structure of the nave seems to repeat itself in a shortened form in the presbytery. Indeed, there first of all follows an appropriately structured bay, which at the top is closed off by a barrel vault with a lunette on each side. But then a large arch leads up to the area of the high altar, which is built on a square ground-plan, and whose importance is emphasised by an increased instrumentation of the area in front of the walls: fluted columns are placed in the corners of the multiple layered pilasters, and the area closes above in a wide stretching cross-vault.

On the east side of the presbytery, Palladio once again takes up the motif of fluted columns in a three-fold, two-storeyed order. The

Below: the campanile (belltower) was added to San Giorgio Maggiore in the eighteenth century. As the counterpart of the great campanile of St. Mark's, it is one further element that fits in with the condition that the complex complement the buildings on St. Mark's Square.

monks' choir, which lies behind it, is both visible through and closed off by a sort of grille screen. Its actual length cannot be measured by the eye. On entering, one sees a rectangular area which merges smoothly into a semi-circle. The walls are structured symmetrically by semicircular shapes in front of them, between which there open up alternately windows and niches. Above the offset ledge, the windows are accentuated by richly profiled gables in the shape of triangles and segmental arches. Michelangelo's principle of as it were turning the arrangement of the outside façades onto the inside appears to have a clear effect here. Below this wall structure, the luxurious seating with Gasparo Gatti's carvings, which were made between 1594 and 1598 – in other words only a few years after the monks' choir was completed – occupies the area of the base.

The architectural richness of this the first of Palladio's monumental church buildings is not merely a question of the great variety of the three-dimensional picture, which opens up along the longitudinal axis. When one reaches the crossways and looks left and right, one sees a transept that is almost independent in its structure, and which nearly outdoes the longitudinal building in the logically consistent development of its detail. One's eyes are guided on both sides from the ends of the transepts which, with their calottes, are built on a semi-circular ground-plan, over a barrel-vaulted rectangular bay on each side to the dome of the crossways, which does not develop its entire effect as the gathering centre until this cross-axis. The way in which dimensions of varying weight are harmonized in the corner pillars becomes apparent from the crossways in a richer and clearer way than it does in the longitudinal view.

The transept, distinctly long as it is, is made to seem even longer by various subtle devices. Palladio shifts the pilasters inwards at the start of the conches. When looking at the neighbouring half-columns, we suspect the gap to be greater than it proves when measured. A similar effect is caused by the completely flat modelling of the pilasters next to the altars in the conches: the contrast of the modelling once again indicates a distance which in reality does not exist at all.

The importance of San Giorgio Maggiore with respect to the developmental history of European architecture can only be compared with that of Michelangelo's new building of St. Peter's in Rome. Palladio offered what was until then an unknown measure of voluminous structuring of the whole and its parts. For the plastic elements are not placed in front of the wall, but rather seem to develop out of it. By enabling the shell of the building actively to release forces, Palladio laid one of the foundations of European Baroque. At the same time, Palladio overcame the assembly of individual parts in favour of a unified area, which while certainly not yet completely realized, was nonetheless clearly recognisable as a goal. Above all, Palladio developed the individual elements of a basic idea common to all parts: this was to be of almost revolutionary importance especially on Venetian territory. Finally, an important step was made on the path to a fusion of longitudinal and centralized buildings, which would occupy the architects of the seventeenth century in so many different ways.

"Those churches that are laid out in a cruciform are also most praiseworthy. Their entrances are in that part which is the foot of the cross. The main altar and choir lie opposite. And there are two further entrances or two further altars in the two transepts, which stretch out on both sides like arms. As this building is built in the shape of a cross, it is meant to bring to the spectator's eye that wood on which is founded the mystery of our salvation. I built the church of San Giorgio Maggiore in Venice in this form."
(Andrea Palladio, 1570)

p. 155: the overall view from the entrance to the choir is richly rhythmical both with regard to the wall structure and the vaulting. The strongly accentuated pillars of the crossing – pilasters, with flanking three-quarter columns, which are set at right angles to each other – lead via round arches that open up equally on all sides up to the dome. Because light also falls through the crowning lantern, the crossways appears as the centre of the building.

Il Redentore

Rio della Croce (Venice)

Towards the end of his life, Palladio was given the opportunity to gather together all his thoughts relating to church building in one stately building. On 4th September 1576, the Senate of Venice decided to found a votive church to the Saviour, in order to deliver the city from a serious outbreak of the plague. A good site was needed. Within a few days, a quickly formed committee suggested the area on the shore of the Giudecca, which faced the Piazzetta di San Marco and which was immediately next to a Capuchin monastery, whose members would take over the task of looking after the future building.

On 23rd November 1576, Palladio received the commission to carry out the work. He was to supply two designs, one on a longitudinal, the other on a "round" ground-plan. Marcantonio Barbaro, the old friend and patron of Palladio's, favoured the project with the "round" ground-plan, in other words, a centralised building such as Baldassare Longhena was to build half a century later, between 1630 and 1687, for a similar reason at the sharply pointed triangle at the confluence of the Grand Canal and the Bacino di San Marco. But on 9th January 1577, the majority of the committee convened to decide about the project pronounced themselves (influenced not least by the decisions of the Council of Trent) in favour of a longitudinal building.

This longitudinal building was better qualified to fulfil the function of a processional, votive and monastery church. As well as that, the aversion of the Counter-Reformation to centralised buildings certainly played a part, for it was said to be a form with heathen characteristics borrowed from the ancients. So Marcantonio Barbaro, four years later, at last gave Palladio the opportunity to realise his ideas of centralised buildings in a smaller format by building the Tempietto near the Villa in Maser.

The foundation stone was laid on 3rd May 1577. On 21st May of the same year, a ceremonial procession took place for the first time, for which a large altar had been erected on the square in front of the church-to-be, and opposite it a theatre-like backdrop raised as a reference to the church to be built. The construction work appears to have come along briskly, although Palladio was not to live to see the completion of his work. The ceremonial consecration was carried out

p. 157: Il Redentore. Ground-plan below and longitudinal section (above) according to Ottavio Bertotti-Scamozzi. Andrea Palladio was supposed to prepare two sketches – a centralised and a longitudinal building – for the church that was to be newly built. Both the influence of the Council of Trent and the fact that the liturgical practice of the Church of Rome established its spatial requirements on the lines of traditional longitudinal buildings must have influenced the decision of the committee responsible in favour of the plan for such a longitudinal building.

on 27th September 1892. The stringboards of the steps and the sculptures on the façade were not added until the second half of the seventeenth century. From 1593 onwards a ceremonial procession took place every year on the third Sunday in July from the palace of the Doge across the Grand Canal and, by means of a pontoon bridge, from the Zattere, the road along the shore line of the main island, across to the new church.

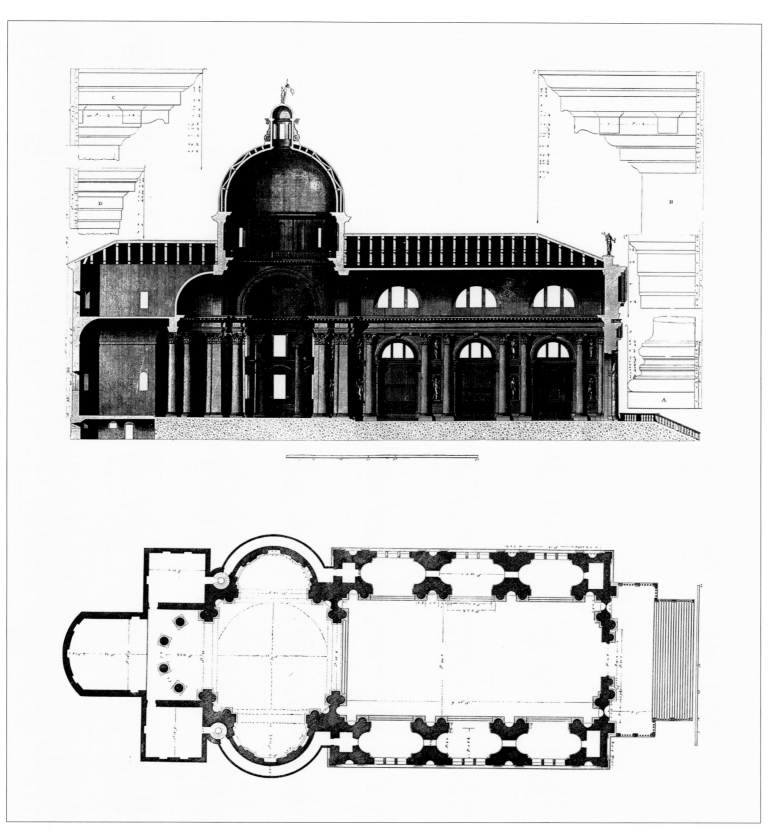

From the point of view of urban development, Palladio saw himself faced with a similar task as with San Giorgio Maggiore: the façade of the new church turned slightly towards the façade of San Giorgio, had to establish the connection across the water to the buildings on the Piazzetta of San Marco. In accordance with this optical amalgamation, Palladio adopted basic motifs from his older creations, but formed a fundamentally new whole out of them. Side parts with the rising beginnings of gables and "temple porticos" with a colossal order and dominating central gables do not stand apparently clear of the end wall of the nave, but in each case have closed wall surfaces behind them. These form a stepped-back second storey which once again ends in rising gable profiles at the sides, but in the middle ends in a horizontal corbel course, above which a sloped roof takes up the directional trend of the gable and leads on to the dome between two small bell-towers. So the façade in its entirety shows itself to be the end wall of a cube arranged in layers. It is not the "temple front" itself with a wall drawn along behind its columns that forms the façade, but just the reverse with a pre-existing wall surface being modelled with the motifs of a temple front.

Just as he already had with the façade of San Francesco della Vigna, Palladio overcame the slight discord between the side axes and the central part which characterizes San Giorgio. He placed the entire façade on one continuous base which corresponds in height to the flight of steps. The intensification of the volume from the sides to the centre is steady and non-contrastive: Palladio takes up the framing of the side parts by pilasters in the more strongly protruding corner pilasters of the "temple front" and thereby creates a transition to the centre columns which are modelled far out of the stone-work as three-quarter columns. The impression of unity is heightened by counterparts in the width of the axes. While comparatively wide side axes stand next to the narrow axes of the "temple front", whose centre is again distinguished by the width and richness of the structure, in both San Giorgio Maggiore and San Francesco della Vigna, in the façade of the Redentore Palladio brings the side parts into line with the side axes of the "temple front" and in return allows the central axis with the portal to dominate all the more emphatically. The restless alternation of wide – narrow – wide – narrow – wide, which characterized previous façades, is now countered by the sequence narrow – narrow – wide – narrow – narrow, which is at the same time a means to heightened unity. It must not be overlooked that the lay-out of the area also plays a part; this argument can however only hold good for San Giorgio Maggiore with its wide side aisles, while in San Francesco della Vigna the low side parts of the façade reach far beyond the row of chapels which flank the nave.

In order to avoid the impression of a temple portico with a wall that closes on to it immediately behind, Palladio resorted to the same means that he had already developed for San Francesco della Vigna: the flanking columns and the gable of the portal are in form and volume brought nearly into line with the colossal order. Here for the first time they take up the entire height of the central column arrange-

p. 158: The church of Il Redentore had to serve three purposes: it was planned as a votive church out of thanks for the deliverance of Venice from the Plague. Moreover, it was the monastery church of the Capuchin monks who had settled on the Giudecca and who were to look after the church. And finally, it was the goal of a procession which had been promised in the vow which led to the building of the church, and which had taken place every year since 21st July 1577.

ment – a further formal method that aims at unity. Accordingly, the façade remains undecorated with the exception of the two figure niches in the side axes of the colossal order. Never before in his commissioned churches had Palladio been able to limit himself so strictly to "pure" architecture.

As Il Redentore rises visible for a considerable distance over the lower buildings on the area that adjoins on both sides, Palladio also gave especial care to the forming of the sides. In the lower storey, the brickwork is arranged into double pilasters with Corinthian capitals, between which there open niches in the lower part of the wall – a foretaste of the arrangement of the walls on the inside. In the upper floor, double revetments form the optical continuation of the pilasters.

When one enters, numerous associations with San Giorgio Maggiore will at first come to mind. In both places there are the many and varied uses of columns in their different plastic shapings of half, three-quarter and full columns, the insertion of arcade arrangements in front of the walls, the barrel vaulting with lunettes over the thermal windows, the flowing of the line of motion into a dominant dome area, and the view through an arrangement of columns into a monks' choir that cannot at first be gauged by the eye.

But the relationship of the individual elements was meant to allow the fundamental different quality of the conception of the space to show itself all the more clearly. First of all, Il Redentore is not a three-aisled basilica, but in the nave a hall with accompanying chapels along the sides. These chapels do not then open towards the centre in a regular sequence, but in the form of the "rhythmical travée"; in other words, a wider opened wall section is followed each time by a narrower closed one. Two triple rhythms interact: the colossal columns that lie in front can be assigned either to the closed wall area or to the chapel openings.

Connection and fusion also characterize the remaining structural elements: Palladio gives up the high pedestals of the colossal half-columns which distinguish the nave of San Giorgio Maggiore in favour of lower right-angled bases, so that the chapels and central area are closer connected. Because the narrow closed areas each contain two niches, one over the other, so that the wall there moves outwards, the motif of the chapel openings is alluded to, and at the same time these niches connect visually with the niches in the transverse walls between the chapels. The interaction of structures in front of the walls, niches and chapels that reach far into the room result in a lovely movement of the wall's relief – a premonition of Baroque solutions, in which the surrounding walls are set swinging alternately back and forth. Palladio did remain, though, in accordance with his era, committed in principle to ordering the details at right angles.

The relationship of the wall and the vaulting is fundamentally changed compared with San Giorgio Maggiore. On the one hand Palladio connects the monumental ledge with the chapel openings by means of volutes, on the other hand he leads the ledge – widened by a multiple profiling to an architrave – around the main area without offsetting it. An immediate connection with the vaulting is not pro-

"The church of Il Redentore, a lovely great work of Palladio's, with a façade more praiseworthy than that of San Giorgio. One has to see these works, which have been reproduced in copperplate engravings many a time, in front of one in order to be able to clarify what has been said. (. . .) He (Palladio) was dissatisfied, as I can conclude from mild phrases in his book, that his contemporaries were continuing to build their Christian churches according to the form of ancient basilicas, and he therefore attempted to bring his sacred buildings closer to the form of ancient temples; this caused certain unseemly features, which appear to have been happily eliminated in Il Redentore, but appear too obviously in San Giorgio . . . Inside, Il Redentore is equally exquisite, everything, even the patterning of the altars, is by Palladio . . ."
(Johann Wolfgang von Goethe, 3rd October 1786, Venice)

160

The church of Il Redentore rises, visible at quite a distance, over the low tops of the buildings on the land on either side. For this reason Palladio shaped the sides of the building especially carefully. Niches open in the lower part of the wall between the pilasters.

duced; indeed, as its start is concealed by the wide architrave, it seems to float – as a continuation of the solution for the dome already seen in San Giorgio Maggiore and in anticipation of the vaulting of the Tempietto in Maser. Instead, the vaulting itself acquires a unity which could hardly yet be foreseen in San Giorgio. In place of the lunettes, carved as sharp-edged triangles that start above the offset pillars there, we here have the spherically curved beginnings of cross-barrel vaulting – once again in the sense of a formal alignment.

Otherwise than in San Giorgio Maggiore, one's eyes are not led directly from the longitudinal axis to the area of the dome. Palladio makes the wall turn in at the end of the nave – corresponding exactly to the inner wall of the façade – to the width of one of the narrow wall areas with which it is, in addition, aligned by means of two niches set into the wall one above the other.

The crossways, incomparably more richly formed than in San Giorgio Maggiore, opens out beyond it: a square with bevelled corners which opens to three sides in somewhat drawn back conches, which are all the same in the ground-plan. The bevelling of the dome area takes over the structure of the narrow travées from the nave: the wall segments between the half-columns open into two niches arranged one above the other.

The radius of the side conches corresponds exactly to the width of the side chapels in the main area – again the close relationship, in which the parts stand to each other, even when, as in this case, this is not immediately apparent to the eye.

The visitor entering the crossways receives the impression of a harmoniously well-ordered centralised building with a lengthened

Left: questions of town planning had to be considered in the structuring of the façade of the church of Il Redentore: the façade of the new church had to make the connection with the buildings across the water on the Piazzetta di San Marco.

west arm. It is possible that impressions Palladio gained during his study of Michelangelo's solution for the choir in St. Peter's in Rome linger on here. In the structure of the arms of the transept, Palladio falls back on the solution which he developed in San Giorgio Maggiore, but improves on the solution realized there by reducing the volume of the structures in front of the walls from almost free-standing pillars to flat pilasters between the windows and by attaining the suggestion of a more widely drawn radius with the aid of this varying "degree of relief".

And not least, the transition from the area of the crossing to the closing monks' choir represents a higher stage in development when compared to San Giorgio Maggiore. Because Palladio rejected the "Baldachin architecture" of the older concept in favour of the semi-circular ground-plan, he on the one hand gained the completed harmony of the dome area, and on the other hand, created a form which fused the area of the high altar with the monks' choir. This is heightened by the permeability of the wall. In principle, Palladio is re-using a motif from the older building: an arrangement of columns forms both the end of the area of the high altar and the way through to the monks' choir. But the relinquishment of the doubling of the columns, and above all of their horizontal subdivision, brings about not only a tighter conjunction but at the same time the consonance of the column orders of crossways and nave. The joining together of the parts is emphasized by the horizontal ledge which surrounds the entirety of a room that is so strongly differentiated.

The problem of the connection of longitudinal and centralised rooms was nowhere solved with the same perfection in the sixteenth century. In Il Redentore, Palladio realised the three-fold function of the building quite easily: the naves as a route for the processions, the three conches as the votive church, the adjoining monks' choir for the liturgical functions of the Capuchin monks charged with its care. Whether a further iconological programme in the sense of an "architecture parlante" ("talking architecture" which illustrates a certain concept) forms the basis of Il Redentore can only be asked with all due caution: the repetition of a three-fold order in the ground-plan and sketch is conspicuous. In correspondence with its function, Il Redentore not only consists of three rooms that are ordered one after the other, are shaped in quite different ways and are nonetheless closely connected to each other, but the number three determines both the structure of the nave and the form of the presbytery. Is this meant to be an allusion to the Holy Trinity? No indications in this direction can be gained from the documents that have been handed down to us.

Leone Battista Alberti's church of San Andrea in Mantua, which was designed in 1470 and points far into the future, remains, despite the differences in their stylistic histories, the model for Palladio's Redentore where developmental history is concerned. Here Palladio was able to find an ideal model of the concept of the great room vaulted by a unified barrel vault, of the system of the "rhythmical travée" with barrel-vaulted side chapels and drawn-in narrow wall surfaces, and of the great importance of a domed crossways. A comparative look also reveals Palladio's independent achievement: the whole not as the sum of its individual parts, but rather the parts as necessary components of the whole; the shell of the room not as the accord of correctly structured surfaces, but as the embodiment of plastically modelled parts, which are passed on to the impression of a "gap"; the directional values not in the careful balance of horizontal and vertical, but directed in favour of the dynamic ascent. Only Michelangelo is the adequate model in the architectural history of the sixteenth century. Once again, in the last years of his life, Palladio crosses the threshold between the late Renaissance and the Baroque.

". . . artificial paradises are beautiful in the imagination alone, they are damned illuminations for the dissatisfied, they are not the thing itself but merely illuminations of the thing, not the façade of a church by Palladio or someone or other but merely the lighting that gives it a supernatural beauty, white and gleaming, whereas in reality the church is a dirty white, old, its paint flaking off, a few architraves damaged, but only as it actually is is it truly beautiful, a thing that is not illuminated but loved."
(Alfred Andersch, The Red, 1960)

Villa Emo

Fanzolo di Vedelago (Treviso)

The building of the Villa Emo in Fanzolo is the stately culmination of a long-lasting endeavour of the Emo family to cultivate the estates on which the villa was built. These efforts can be traced back to 1509. In that year, which saw the defeat of Venice by the League of Cambrai, the extensive property, which belonged to the Villa Emo, changed ownership. It was Leonardo di Giovanni Emo who purchased the property from the Barbarigo family. A mansion was also part of this property.

Leonardo's central interest was at first in the cultivation of the

Ground-plan and elevation from the Quattro Libri. The farming wings are bordered on the left and right sides by small towers, so-called columbaries (dove-cotes). Doves, which were usually destined to end up on the villa owner's table, found shelter here. From an aesthetic point of view, the columbaries take on the task of giving the mansion a vertical counter-emphasis.

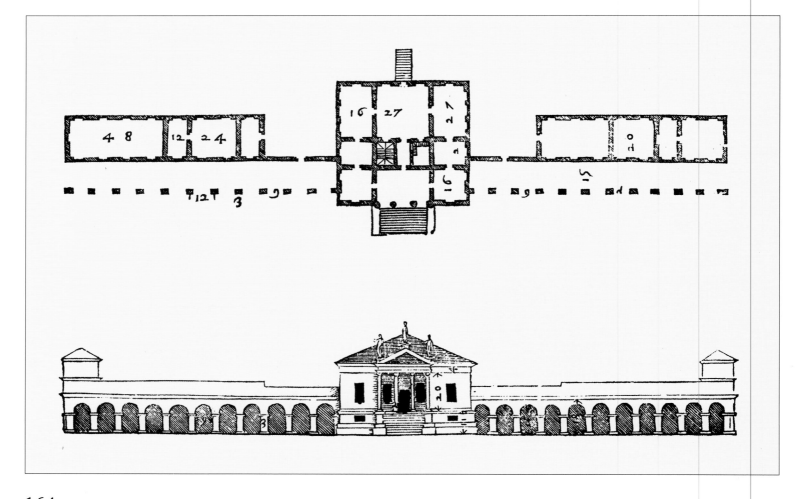

ground in the region. Not until two generations had passed did Leonardo di Alvise Emo commission Palladio to build a new villa in Fanzolo. We unfortunately do not have any dates which could give us information as to the start on the new building.

The year 1555 is assumed to be the date of the start of the work, while the date of the end of the work is put at 1565; a document which attests to the marriage of Leonardo di Alvise with Cornelia Grimani has come down to us from that year.

Andrea Palladio emphasises the usefulness of the lay-out in his *Quattro Libri*. He points out that the grain stores and work areas of the villa are accommodated both to the left and right of the mansion house and could be reached under cover, which was particularly important. Also, it was necessary for the Villa Emo's size to correspond to the

Right: The Villa Emo was built as an agriculturally functional estate. However, what was more important than the building of the mansion was the cultivation of the ground of the surrounding area, which had been in the hands of the Emo family since 1509. The Villa Emo was built only once this task had been completed as a symbol of economic prosperity.

pp. 166/167: the mansion, which is raised above ground level, attains a commanding majesty in its simple forms. The shadowy arch arrangements support a rhythm which leads from the outermost boundaries of the farming wings towards the mansion, and receives its greatest intensification there. So the farming wings and the mansion form a homogeneous unity.

165

Above left: the columbaries, which flank the farm wings, form a vertical counter-stress to the mansion and give the grounds a self-contained appearance.

Above right: the "temple front" had in the meantime become a firm component of Palladio's formal idiom. It alludes both to the villa ideal of "holy agriculture" and to the dignity of the owner.

p. 168: the extensive arcades tell of the wealth of the Emo family. High yields, which were stored in the farming wings, could be achieved by the cultivation of maize. The arcades in front of these farming wings were for the convenience of the head of the household: even if it were to rain, he would be able to reach his store rooms without getting wet.

returns obtained by good management. These returns must in fact have been considerable, for the side wings of the building are unusually long, a visible symbol of their prosperity. This assumption of the fertility of the fields belonging to the villa is confirmed when we bear in mind the fact that the Emo family introduced the cultivation of maize on their estate. In contrast to the traditional cultivation of millet, considerably higher returns could be obtained this way.

The outer appearance of the Villa Emo is marked by a simple treatment of the entire body of the building, whose structure is determined by a geometrical rhythm. In its pure form, it embodies the functional building born of the idea of "holy agriculture", which, being subordinated to its purpose, dispenses with grandeur and still represents the heart of the villa complex. The function of the mansion can already be recognised in that it is raised above ground-level, as are all of Palladio's other villas. A wide flight of steps leads up to the loggia; the temple front – a column portico crowned by a gable – which was applied to secular buildings henceforth became a permanent element in Palladio's formal repertoire, and mirrors the dignity of the owner of the villa. As is the case with the Villa Badoer, the loggia does not stand out from the core of the building as an entrance hall, but is retracted into it. The emphasis on simplicity extends to the column order of the loggia, for which Palladio chose the extremely plain Tuscan order.

Nonetheless, the hierarchical layering of the individual villa compartments is preserved here. As can already be observed at the Villa Badoer, the farming wings, in contrast to the mansion house, are not raised above ground level. These farming wings end externally on both sides in receding dove-cotes, called columbaries, which tower above the farming wings. The apparently interminable row of them away from the mansion house is checked by this vertical stress, indeed is almost reversed. The dynamic tension does not come from the mansion house and subside at the sides, but starts at the columbaries in order to develop its entire potential force, which is at first somewhat weakened by the farming wings, in the mansion house. The farming wings are characterized by a row of arch arrangements which prepare us visually for the motif of the portico and strengthen its effect.

Such visual experiences can only be derived from a personal point of view, though; Palladio's own comments on such observations can for understandable reasons not be found in the descriptions of the buildings he created. Most of his villas came into being at a time in which Venice once again needed money to an increased degree for future wars, and as a result enacted laws against luxury. Furthermore, Palladio's architectural treatise appeared in 1570, one year before the

p. 171: a series of frescoes in the Villa Emo is grouped around the area with scenes featuring Venus, the goddess of Love. Giambattista Zelotti appears to have begun work on the frescoes in 1565.

Below: the area upon which the Villa Emo was built was previously a marsh. Leonardo di Giovanni Emo acquired this area in 1509 and started, possibly on the advice of Alvise Cornaro, to reclaim land from the marsh.

p. 172: in the great room of the Villa Emo, the events on the frescoes concentrate on humanistic ideals. Exemplary scenes of illustrated prudence, or as in this detail, Virtue, are portrayed by a scene from the life of Scipio.

Right: another room in the villa is called the Room of the Arts. The frescoes in this hall are allegories of individual arts, such as astronomy, poetry or music.

pp. 174/175: the abstinence of Scipio, which is the theme of this fresco in the great room of the Villa Emo, appears frequently in cycles of frescoes for Venetian villas, for instance in the Villa Porto Colleoni in Thiene, or, nearly two hundred years later, in the Villa Cordellina in Montecchio Maggiore. In them ideals which had in the fifteenth and sixteenth centuries resulted from the renewed discussion of the depravity of town life became a part of current thinking.

Battle of Lepanto. His deliberate action when describing the utility of his buildings served both his clients and himself, the architect who moreover applied for the post of the first architect in Venice. Instead, a splendour that is all the greater unfolds inside the villas; this was also the case in the Villa Emo, whose frescoes have come down to us in an excellent state of preservation. These frescoes can be traced back to Giambattista Zelotti. Here too an allegorical scenario of ancient mythology is seen in a copious abundance, framed by an extremely differentiated sham architecture and thought of as the glorification of the ideal of "vita in villa".

Palazzo Valmarana

Corso Fogazzaro 16 (Vicenza)

The consideration of Andrea Palladio's town palaces raises great problems. The Palazzo Chiericati was fortunately completed, albeit late; but there were many which were either never completed or whose plans had to be hastily altered. On the whole one can start with the assumption that the palace façades are most likely to correspond to the original designs. Where the ground-plans are concerned, one must refer to the sketches in the *Quattro Libri*, which were certainly published in an idealised form for the most part. A fundamental reason for this situation appears to have been Venice's economic crisis of around 1570, which also included the Terraferma and led to a sudden stop of the building work on Palladio's palaces during this time.

The Plazzo Valmarana, which we are now going to consider, poses similar problems. The foundation stone was laid in 1566. This can be established with certainty, as a commemorative medallion dating from that year was found in the process of renovation work in the nineteenth century, and tells of the laying of this foundation stone. It is nonetheless necessary, with regard to the history of the building, to look back almost a hundred years before that time. A will of Stefano Valmarana's that was drafted in 1487 and is kept in the Padua town archives has come down to us which gives us information about his ownership of a house with a courtyard and garden. This property was situated exactly where the Palazzo Valmarana now stands. Benedetto Valmarana, Stefano's heir, sold this property in 1493, thereby disregarding the provisions in Stefano's will. A large house, courtyard, vegetable garden and additional garden are mentioned in the deed of sale.

Referring to Stefano Valmarana's will, at the beginning of the sixteenth century Benedetto's immediate heirs took legal action and demanded the return of the sold property, and they got it back (this information was made available to research by Lionello Puppi). In 1565 an alteration of the property was decided upon. It had probably already been planned by Giovanni Alvise Valmarana; but the driving force behind the start to the venture was his widow, Isabella Nogarola. Giovanni Alvise's son, Leonardo, whom Palladio names as the client, was still a minor in 1566, six years after his father's death (he is assumed to have been born about 1548). But both the completion of

"In the above-named town, the Counts Valmarana, most worthy noblemen, have also built to the following designs for their own honour and for the benefit and decoration of their native town. This building does not lack much decoration, such as stucco work and paintings. This house is divided in two parts by a courtyard in its centre, around which there is a walkway or balcony, by which one can reach the front part of the rear building . . . The garden, which is situated in front of the stables, is very much larger than shown here. But we had to draw it this small, as otherwise the paper would not have been big enough to include the stables and other parts too."
(Andrea Palladio, 1570)

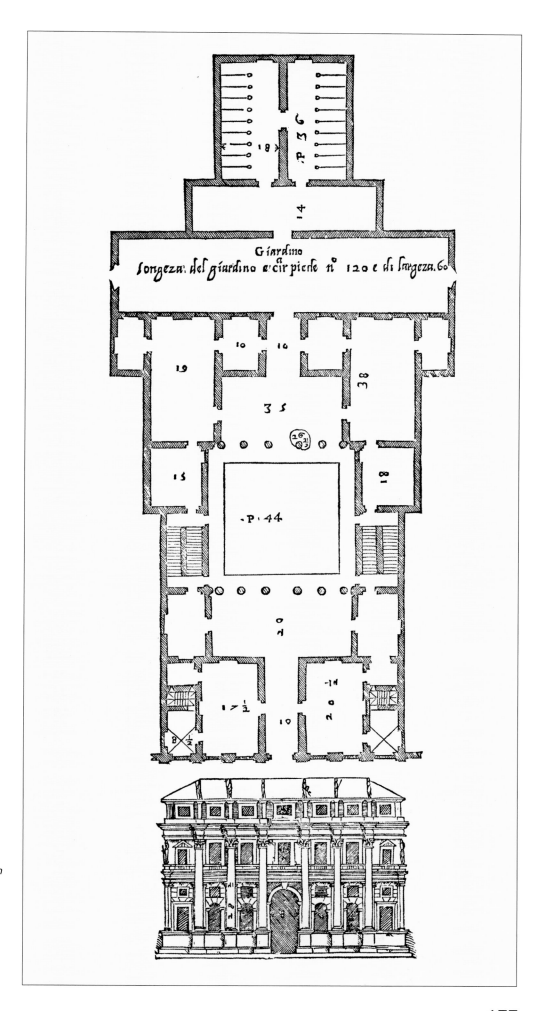

Giardino

Longeza: del giardino e cir piede nᵒ 120 e di largeza. 60

Ground-plan and elevation from the Quattro Libri. In the ground-plan's lay-out, Palladio achieved an exceedingly rich differentiation in the opening out of the rooms. The shaping of the façade is also one of the outstanding plans of Palladio's creative work. In contrast to his earlier palaces, the vertical structure of the façade is also reflected in the arrangement of the ground-plan. The rows of rooms are arranged along two continuous longitudinal axes.

the work and its artistic decoration can be traced back to him. The execution of the Palazzo Valmarana does however also differ considerably from Andrea Palladio's plan. Leonardo was obviously not willing – no doubt for financial reasons, among others – to allow all the already existing buildings to be torn down, just in order to smooth the way for the carrying out of Palladio's plan. Rather, bordering buildings were adapted to the requirements. The agricultural rooms were accommodated in the outbuildings of the old palace.

The construction work appears to have been completed in 1582. A plaque over the entrace portal tells of a visit by Mary of Austria, who was accommodated along with her retinue in the Palazzo Valmarana in the September of the same year. The final condition of the building shows that only the façade was carried out in accordance with Palladio's plan. Only the lower half of the ground-plan was completed.

This ground-plan deserves a closer examination, even though it was only partially carried out. Andrea Palladio published his plan of the Palazzo Valmarana as a ground-plan and sketch of the façade in the *Quattro Libri*. Nonetheless, an idealisation such as has already been established elsewhere can also be observed here. At no stage of his planning could Palladio reckon with the realisation of a plan which placed the surrounding walls at right angles to each other. The bend in the street that the façade faces on to made the implementation of such a design impossible from the start. Nevertheless, his endeavour to conceive the ground-plan of his buildings with symmetrical axes once again becomes clear. The lay-out of the design follows the requirements of town architecture. Newly-built palaces, like other buildings, normally had to be tied into already existing rows of houses. In order for them still to achieve a stately size, they had to stretch far backwards. So the courtyard, which had to assist the influx of light, was not only a motif borrowed from antiquity, but was an indispensable aid to the structure.

In his design, Palladio made use of the condition of the property. As has already been mentioned, the property of the Valmarana counts contained, apart from the two buildings, both a courtyard and a vegetable garden. Both are clearly integrated in Palladio's design. He arranged a living area between the courtyard and the garden. This was made possible by the existence of the vegetable garden, which according to Palladio was rather longer than the wood engraving published in the *Quattro Libri* suggests. Palladio excuses the reduction in scale by saying that the sheet of paper that it was to be printed on was not large enough, which would otherwise have meant it not being possible to reproduce the entire complex. In any case, Palladio was able to make use of this double possibility for supplying the rooms with light when planning his ground-plan. The arrangement of the Palazzo Valmarana's ground-plan appears to be considerably less complicated when compared to the Palazzo Iseppo Porto, which was built seventeen years earlier. The commitment to the preconditions of the ancients, which had in Palladio's opinion made the integration of a peristyle courtyard necessary there, had now been overcome. Form was now subordinated to purpose, so that an arrangement of six

p. 178: here is the first example of Palladio's use of a colossal order of pilasters on the façade of one of his town palaces. The wall is multiply layered backwards. Its demarcatory character is thereby made unclear. When he was planning the façade, Palladio considered how to incorporate the Palazzo in the already existing street row: the colossal order is given up at the outermost axes. The pilasters there are continued in the piano nobile by so-called telamons.

columns would be used only on two opposite sides of the courtyard. The already relatively simple Ionic order of the piantereno on the courtyard façade was a further step in fitting the decoration of the physical conditions. The sequence of the columns is not regular. The space after the third column is wider than that between the other columns. How much this fits in with Palladio's endeavour to give the ground-plan a dynamic expressive content will subsequently become clear. As is typical of nearly all Palladio's plans, the Palazzo Valmarana too is characterized by the strict binding into a vertical axis scheme (the Palazzo Thiene represents an exception in this context), which has no horizontal directional impulse set against it. This makes the depth of the palace clear and strengthens its intensity. Nonetheless, we are not dealing simply with a concatenation of rooms (at no time in his work did Palladio bear this Renaissance scheme in mind), but rather with a specifically conceived development of the rooms.

The visitor enters the palace through the narrow entrance hall, which is not (as for example in the Palazzo Chiericati) merged with the row of rooms. Leading directly into the courtyard, its counterpart lies on the opposite side of that courtyard, a hall which was meant to have led between the residential wings which meet there through to the garden. The six columns in the courtyard of the completed part are all freestanding. On the opposite side, two rooms had been intended to project from the core of the building, thereby narrowing the courtyard loggia. The two outer columns, whose sequence would have been just as irregular as those opposite them, would then have had to be incorporated into the core of the building.

*MARIA, AUSTRIA.CAROLI V. MASSIMIL.II. RODULPH II.IMP.FILIA.UXOR. ET MATER. A.PHILIPPO. FRATRE. HISPANIARUM.REGE. POTENTISS. AD. REGENDUM.E.GERMANIA. ADSCITA.PER ITALIAM.ITER.FACIENS.IN.HIS. AEDIBUS.QUOD.IPSA.IN. VETEREM.AUSTRIANORUM.PRINCIPUM. ERGA.HANC. DOMUM.CLIENTELAM.MAXIME.VOLUIT.CUM.MARGARETA.MAXIMILIANOQUE. FILIIS.ARCHIDUCHIBUS.A. LEONARDO. VALMARANA.COMITE.EIUSDEMQUE. PHILIPPI.REGIS.PENSIONARIO. SPLENDIDISSIMO.APPARATU.ACCEPTA. FUIT.
ANNO MDLXXXI VII KAL.OCT.*

These observations are not being introduced without a reason. We can now imagine the impression that the rooms would have made had they been carried out in accordance with the plan. In the entrance hall, because of the way the entrance hall was separated from the organism of the building, the two rows of rooms would have appeared as separate wings with a clear longitudinal alignment. The enlargement of the spatial impression would have occurred gradually, first of all by the wider central intercolumniation of the column arrangement in the courtyard. The central axis would have been the most extreme factor in determining the spatial impression in the courtyard: the lack of a column arrangement along the sides would have given it an intensity which would have created the impression that that was pressing the residential wings into the side wings. At the end of the courtyard a visual tightening would have resulted from the slightly advanced body of the building, a tightening which would have positively forced the dynamism of the central axis through the narrow passage, without being able to work against the impression of its intensity. That would, in summary, have meant the inversion of a traditional relationship. The central axis would not have been the result of the two-winged palace lay-out; rather it would have been just the opposite, with the impression being created that the lay-out of the building wings had emerged (as was attempted in Mannerist architecture) from the power which was inherent in this axis and as it were pushed towards the sides. This looks fascinating in the plan; and the actual execution of this plan, which already ended behind the first column arrangement in the courtyard, is regrettable.

The inscription over the portal of the Palazzo Valmarana tells of an occurrence in 1581: The Empress Mary of Austria, the daughter of Charles V, wife of Maximilian II and mother of Rudolph II, was accommodated with a large retinue in this palace belonging to Leonardo Valmarana in the September of 1581. So the palace must both have been finished and complete with representative decorations at this time. In the Second World War, the Palazzo Valmarana was the victim of a bombing raid, but was however restored again.

Andrea Palladio: detail of a drawing of the façde of the Palazzo Valmarana, from the Quattro Libri. When designing a palace for Giacomo Angarano, Palladio had already opted for a row of colossal columns on a street façade. The Palazzo Valmarana saw colossal columns of this kind not only planned but also becoming reality, for the first time in Palladio's career.

That various attempts have been made to describe this ground-plan concept as Mannerist can only stem from a misunderstanding of Palladio's intentions. The idea of designing an inner room from the structure of the façade outside, as was attempted in the architecture of Mannerism, in order to thereby reverse the existing relationship of inside and outside, forms the basis neither of this nor of any other of Palladio's ground-plans and played no part in Palladio's thinking. The exciting relationship of tightening and opening, the organisation of the room lay-out that this requires and the way it is made visible in the body of the building all show Palladio to be the forerunner of Baroque forms of expression rather than an architect who took contemporary formal thinking to a state of aesthetic perfection. The extremely dynamic sketch of the ground-plan of the Palazzo Valmarana is in this sense the application of a new understanding of the treatment of buildings to a ground-plan, an understanding that took shape increasingly on Palladio's façades also, namely the making visible of a force which constituted the body of the building. During the Renaissance, a mutual accord of the supporting and the heavy parts of the building was prevalent, and this relationship was reversed in Mannerist architecture; but meanwhile a concept evolved in which the supporting parts of the building's body were assigned a dominating function. In this sense, the façade of the Palazzo Valmarana presents the latter, as an extremely modern building for which models were understandably entirely lacking in the time around 1565.

The dominance of the supporting power on the façade of the Palazzo Valmarana is revealed first and foremost by six colossal pilasters, which overlap the two storeys of the palace and carry a strongly projecting Attic storey, on which the mezzanine storey rests. These pilasters stand on a continuous building base which is offset as pedestals underneath the pilasters, which stand at ground level and are framed by rusticated stone blocks. In the vertical arrangement of the façade, the pilasters present the most strongly protruding structural element, from which the wall surfaces are staggered backwards in an extremely complex fashion. Through the choice of colossal pilasters in place of a colossal column arrangement as intended in the planning stage, the Palazzo Valmarana is given an exposed position in the street; at the same time it is integrated with houses that were already standing. Consequently, in place of the rhythmical swelling of a colossal column order, there appears the static calm of the pilaster order, which corresponds to the strict vertical structure of the neighbouring buildings. The two outer bays of the façade show just how hard Palladio worked to integrate the Palazzo Valmarana in the street row. The colossal order of the pillars is given up here. Rather, the corner pilasters only reach up to the top ledge of the piantereno, and give way in the piano nobile to sculptures of warriors which support the projecting ledge of the Attic storey. In this way the colossal order of the Palazzo Valmarana is organically changed to the double storey order of the neighbouring buildings.

This change in the order of the storeys corresponds to the windows in the two outer segments of the façade. Both in the piantereno and the piano nobile, the storey windows are smaller than in the rest of the façade. The vertical movement of the palace façade is checked in two ways in these façade segments: a very shadowy mezzanine window appears in the rusticated piantereno above the window – from which it is separated by means of a small three-layered ledge – in place of the relief areas, which are set in the wall above the remaining four windows of the storey. In the piano nobile the windows of the outer bays are the only ones to end in a triangular gable. So while the strict colossal structure of the façade is opposed with regard to those shadowy elements, the parts of the façade that these segments enclose are completely subordinated to the dominance of the colossal pilasters.

The delimitation of the storeys is expressed by a strongly divided ledge which is cut through by the pilasters. In order to set up a system of support that will bear the piano nobile within the core of the building in addition to the pilasters which carry the Attic storey, further pilasters are placed in the piantereno next to the colossal pilasters, and their capitals bear the storey ledge. A further arrangement of the system of pilasters that is carried out in smooth stone blocks complicates the system of support even more: it supports the mezzanine area of the piantereno that is characterized by the relief squares, and at the same time forms the frame of the windows in that storey.

It is worth mentioning that the individual arrangements of pilasters, as the weight that they have to bear becomes less, recede ever more strongly into the wall, thereby layering the latter backwards. This endeavour not to work against the vertical movement is continued in the piano nobile. The windows are only weakly profiled and their height is extended up to the ledge of the Attic storey. The balusters underneath them are limited to the width of the windows and thereby support the vertical structure of the façade, in which their projection and the receding of the windows that this involves correspond to the layering of the wall in the piantereno. The base and the Attic storey can be identified and experienced as horizontal values.

In this connection, the strong projection of the ledge in the Attic storey can be seen as the answer to the area of the base, which protrudes from the core of the building to an equal degree.

The forces which support the building are displayed all too obviously, while all the other parts of the façade are incorporated in this field of influence. On the other hand, the weight to be supported, taken as a structural element, has almost completely faded in importance on the façade on the Palazzo Valmarana, and is bereft of any visual effectiveness.

Palladio always proved to be exceedingly imaginative when it came to incorporating his buildings into their surroundings. This is clearly demonstrated by the fact that he refrained from using a row of colossal columns at the palace corners as would normally have been logical.

Palazzo Schio

Contrada San Marco 39 (Vicenza)

Andrea Palladio started his work on shaping the façade of the Palazzo Schio in 1565 and probably already finished it in 1566. The commission for this work on the palace (which was already being lived in) derived from a provision in the will of Bernardo Schio.

The show side that Palladio was to shape was relatively narrow and contained only three axes.

A comparison of the present condition of the palace with drawings by the architects Francesco Muttoni and Ottavio Bertotti-Schamozzi makes clear the divergence from a condition which obviously still existed in the eighteenth century: a sequence of three mezzanine windows was still arranged over the windows of the piano nobile. Their function was to guide light to a grain store behind it. These mezzanine windows were walled up in 1825. But their previous existence allows Palladio's intentions when shaping the palace façade to be clearly revealed.

Though the façade of the piano nobile is divided up with geometrical rigour, the endeavour to avoid unarticulated wall surfaces can nonetheless be clearly seen. In order to realise this organically, Palladio broke the wall surfaces down to several layers of depth. First of all, four three-quarter columns of the Corinthian order, whose bases are tied in with the rustication of the basement storey, are placed in front of the wall surface. In the spaces between the columns there are three windows, whose bottom ledges rest upon the base storey. In order not to disturb the impression of a correct connection of the windows with the stone-work, balusters are placed in front of the windows. The area between window and architrave is filled by a triangular gable which projects strongly out of the wall. The profiles of the windows also stand out from the wall, thus casting shadows. Consequently, the light which falls onto the palace façade becomes a vital element in the structure, as the still remaining wall surfaces are modelled by the shadows falling on them. The mezzanine windows which used to exist would probably have heightened this effect still further. Palladio took away from them their more or less subordinated rôle on the façade by allowing them to extend out of their storey and break through into the architrave.

A view into the courtyard of the Palazzo Schio. The work in the courtyard cannot be ascribed to Palladio. Palladio was only meant to form the façade for Bernardo Schio's palace. The sculptures in the two niches are of a later date. The crowning of the portal, which is twined around with ivy and which consists of a prominent gable supported by scroll-work, indicates a later date of origin for the courtyard.

Of the work on the Palazzo Schio, only the shaping of the façade can be attributed to Andrea Palladio. Because the palace had to be inserted between two already existing buildings, the representative side that faces the road turned out a bit narrow, with three axes. Palladio's development towards more dynamic palace façades nonetheless becomes clearly visible.

The rusticated base storey is set off against the piano nobile. Here also, to the same extent as in the piano nobile, the light is included as a structural element. As in the piano nobile, the wall is divided into two layers: the star-shaped border of the cellar windows, which is united into one block, stands out underneath the lower window ledges.

The dynamic effect of the palace façade was further intensified in that Palladio avoided the monotony of layering the long and short bosses into horizontal stripes, and dealt with them in a picturesque fashion by using them to echo the form which enclosed them, and making them break out of the horizontal structure, as is especially visible on the portal.

La Rotonda

(Vicenza)

No other villa of Palladio's won admiration from contemporaries and following generations to an equal degree as the Villa Rotonda. Situated south-east of Vicenza in the hill region of the Monte Berico, it seems to grow directly out of the landscape: the façades, which are the same on all four sides and have porticos, take up the rising level of the ground in the flights of steps; the central dome is to be understood as an elevation over the hilltop. Does the centralised building form the culmination of the area – or, the other way round, does the hill grow through into the building?

Palladio himself pointed out the close connection of landscape and building in his *Quattro Libri del' Architettura*: "The place is nicely situated and one of the loveliest and most charming that one could hope to find; for it lies on the slopes of a hill, which is very easy to reach. The loveliest hills are arranged around it, which afford a view into an immense theatre . . .; because one takes pleasure in the beautiful view on all four sides, loggias were built on all four façades." So on the one hand the close blending, indeed fusion, of landscape and architecture is characteristic, and on the other hand this building, which was built according to strict proportions and embodies the idea of the centralised building in a complete manner, stands as a "pure" creation of art in contrast to evolved nature. Concrete things, or nature, and abstract things, i. e. precisely thought out architectural forms, contrast with each other. On a first level, the Villa Rotonda represents, in this tension, a work of Mannerism.

Clarification of the history of its origin is made more difficult in two ways: firstly, there are no definite documents about the execution of the building, and secondly, none of Palladio's plans have come down to us.

The ground-plan and sketch, which he reproduced in his *Quattro Libri* in 1570, show considerable differences from the existing building and can already be regarded as an editing of the plan of the villa, which at that time was not yet completed in all parts.

All the same, it has been possible to establish a general consensus as to the time of building, and with it its classification in the history of the development of Palladio's work. Earlier a date of origin of about 1550

p. 187: ground-plan and elevation of the Villa Rotonda from the Quattro Libri. The Villa Rotonda stands on a square ground-plan. Narrow corridors lead from the loggias up to the main hall of the Rotonda, which is built on a circular ground-plan. In contrast to the remaining rooms, the hall takes up the entire height of the building core and is closed off at the top by the villa's dome.

pp. 188/189: "The place is nicely situated and one of the loveliest and most charming that one could find; for it lies on the slopes of a hill, which is very easy to reach. The loveliest hills are arranged around it, and afford a view into an immense theatre . . .; because one takes pleasure in the beautiful views on all four sides, loggias were built on all four façades." (A. Palladio, 1570)

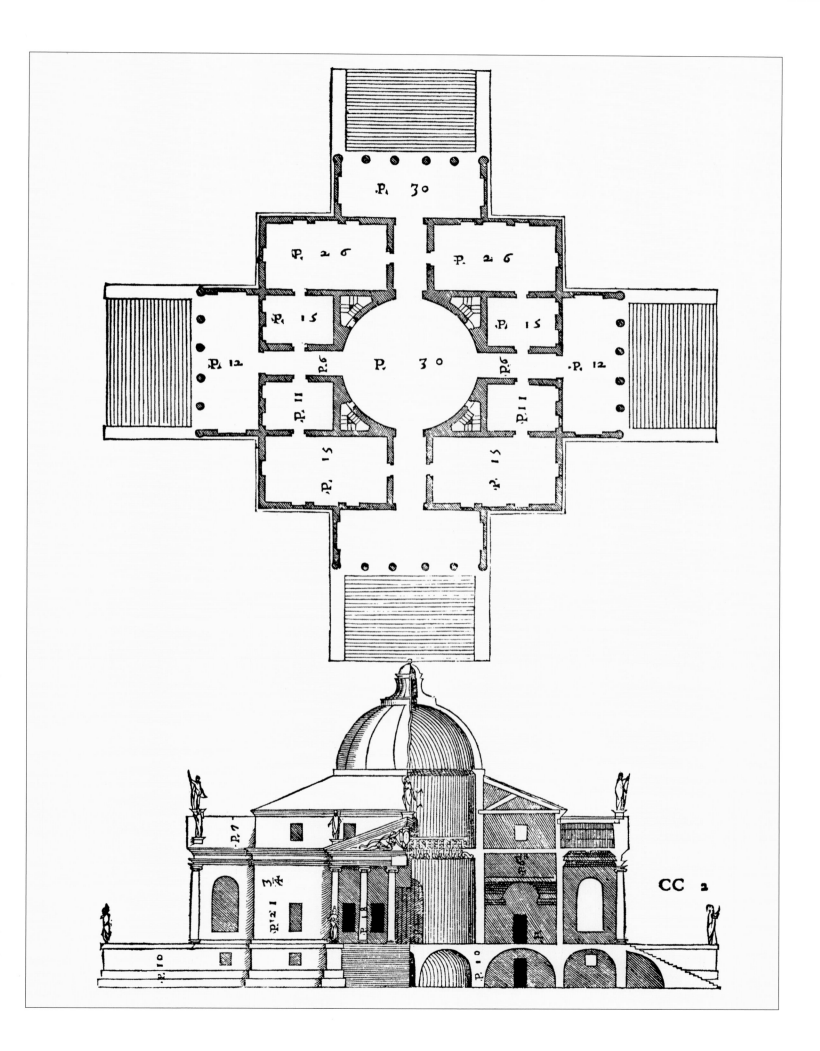

.P. 30

.P. 26   .P. 26

.P. 15   .P. 15

.P. 12   .P. 6   .P. 30   .P. 6   .P. 12

.P. 11   .P. 11

.P. 15   .P. 15

CC 2

had been assumed, as a document states that Count Paolo Almerico had given a magnificent banquet for Lucrezia Gonzago in 1553 "at his delightful place on a hill outside Vicenza." As he had apparently had to wait three years for this meeting, a date of origin of about, or even before, 1550 could be assumed. This piece of information was admittedly non-conclusive, as the family owned extensive lands in this area and as the banquet could perfectly well have taken place in a small and less lavish building.

More decisive is the fact that Giorgio Vasari, the famed biographer of Italian artists from Cimabue to his own time, gathered news during a stay in Venice and the surrounding area in 1566, in which Palladio's works, not least the town palaces of Vicenza, also appear. The Villa Rotonda is not mentioned, though. Such an outstanding work could not have escaped Vasari's notice. In addition, Palladio himself mentions the canon Paolo Almerico from Vicenza as being the client for the

Left: an inscription on one of the four loggias identifies Marius Capra as the owner of the villa. The Rotonda belonged to the Almerico family for only a generation. Because no agricultural concern belonged to it, it was scarcely possible to raise the funds to cover the considerable costs. The son of the villa's commissioner had to sell the Rotonda. The new owner annexed an agricultural business to it, whose farm buildings were built just below the villa.

p. 191: the Villa Rotonda is situated in the vicinity of Vicenza. Palladio mentions in his description that it is at a distance of fewer than four miles from the centre. "Because of its closeness to the town, I did not think that it was suitable to put the drawing in amongst the villas, for one could even say that it lies in the town itself." (Andrea Palladio, 1570)

190

View through one of the four column entrance halls of the Rotonda. Towards the end of the sixteenth century, the importance of gardens for the villas grew. In the course of their growing esteem, they were decorated with fountains, labyrinths and sculptures. At the beginning of the seventeenth century, Agostino Rubini created the sculptural decorations of the Rotonda.

The extent to which Palladio's ideas were faithfully carried out is also disputed.

We know that the small rooms on the Attic storey, at the same height as the triangular gables, were not built until some time between 1725 and 1740. Had they not been planned from the outset, it would be possible to imagine the dome with a more dominant effect than it now has. On the other hand, Palladio's sketch in his *Quattro Libri* already has this Attic storey. The shape of the completed dome is also greatly different from the drawing that Palladio published: now stepped down in various rings, in Palladio's drawing it is a half-sphere, whose outlines are pulled tight, completed by a lantern.

We have to start with the present appearance of the building. It is a cube built over a square ground-plan, with column porticos, which are all shaped exactly the same, placed in front of it on all four sides, thus widening the complete outline to the shape of a Greek cross.

192

The design of this group of sculptures based on a theme from the life of Heracles (Roman: Hercules). The Greek demi-god is depicted with a goat on his arm. That a group of sculptures with this theme was put up becomes understandable when we on the one hand consider that, at the time that the sculptural programme was carried out, the Rotonda already belonged to the Capra family, and on the other hand that the Italian word "capra" simply means a goat.

Wide flights of steps, each with about twenty steps, lead between horizontal stringboards up to the column arrangement, which on all sides projects far into the garden. Palladio here uses once again the motif of an arcade on massive pillars which protrudes from the wall at right angles, against which each of the corner columns stands out freely. Of the five intercolumniations, the central one is accentuated by being slightly wider. Its counterpart on the walls of the cubical main building is the richly profiled and gabled main portal. The modelled and strongly protruding door gables are connected with the frames at the sides of the doors by elegantly sweeping volutes. The accompanying openings, windows drawn down nearly to floor level, are cut simply into the surface of the walls in the axis of the side column arrangements.

Palladio chose the Ionic order for his porticos, whose capitals with volutes rolled up at the sides lead from the vertical line of the columns to the horizontal line of the ledge and the base of the triangular gable.

The inscription plaques over the central column arrangements refer to Count Capra, who bought the Villa in 1591, and are therefore later additions. The gables, which are framed by a powerful console profile, each open out into two horizontally oval windows, which frame a coat of arms.

As always, Palladio connects the individual parts of the building by formal correspondences or parallels. The ledge between the portico columns and the triangular gables is continued around the building, and Palladio again strongly emphasizes the smoothly sweeping profile in a way which has been familiar since the "basilica". The windows in the wall surfaces next to the front of the columns take over the framing of the main portals – on the one hand the connection of the portico and the wall surfaces, on the other that of the walls which are at right angles to each other. The base storey, whose height is continued by the walls at the sides of the steps, approximately corresponds both in height and windowing to the Attic storey, but certainly, in its function as the base for the entire building, appears more massive due to a simply layered profile.

The proportions and principles become clear in the ground-plan with positively mathematical precision. The porticos take up half the width of the cubical central building. The column entrance halls and flights of steps each correspond to half the depth of the core of the building. In other words: the sum of the four porticos and flights of steps covers the same area as the main building. (Goethe, on 21st September 1786, noted down the facts of the matter, even exaggerating somewhat: "The area that the steps and entrance halls take up is far

Below left: the ancient world is evoked in many ways in the sculptural programme. The Villa Rotonda is also no exception to this. The youth holding a lyre is possibly a portrayal of Orpheus.

Below right: Two further sculptures, which are situated on a parapet to the side of the Rotonda's entrance.

Several sculptors were involved in the sculptural programme of the Villa Rotonda. Palladio himself mentions the master who made the sculptures on the outer ends of the pedestals, which support the steps of the loggia, in his Quattro Libri as being Lorenzo Vicentino.

larger than that of the house itself: for each individual side would be satisfactory as the front view of a temple.") A narrow barrel-vaulted passage leads from each side into a central room built on a circular ground-plan, whose diameter corresponds to the width of the column porticos, that is, half a side of the square main building. Rectangular rooms are ordered in a regular sequence around the central domed room.

The external view, ground-plan and cross-section of the Villa Rotonda seem to embody the ideal of the centralized building in a purity which the High Renaissance often dreamt of but rarely realised. The surprise of the visitor entering the domed room is all the greater. While the middle of the centralised lay-out is once again emphasized by a lion's head, let into the floor, from which alternately red and white

Right: while the great hall of the Rotonda is the same height as the entire core of the building, it is however structured horizontally by a balustrade, which corresponds to the storey division of the remaining rooms. Because it is situated in the middle of the building, this room is however nearly entirely reliant upon artificial lighting. Natural light can only reach the room through the four corridors, which connect it with the loggias.

p. 196: the themes of the frescoes in the lower area of the great hall in the Villa Rotonda are borrowed from ancient mythology. Echoing the representative function of the villa, no scenes of "vita in villa" are depicted here, but individual ancient gods (such as Zeus, the Roman Jupiter, to the left next to the door).

patterns radiate like the spokes of a wheel, the impression of a centre that gathers all the forces in itself fails to come across: without any direct light the room remains dark, the almost shaft-like corridors on all four sides invevitably draw one's eyes outwards in the direction of the light. In place of centripetal forces, for which both the whole and the details seem to be planned, there appear on the contrary centrifugal impulses of movement. Comparable with the tense relationship between nature and art in the external view, Palladio interprets a classical principle in a strictly anti-classical sense in the disposition of rooms inside his Villa Rotonda.

How far the superabundant decoration of sculptures and paintings would have corresponded to Palladio's intentions is something we do not know. Palladio was still alive when Lorenzo Rubini's statues were set up on the stringboards (presumably before 1570, because they are already indicated in Palladio's drawings in the *Quattro Libri*). The stucco ornaments in the domed room and on the ceilings are attributed to the workshop community of Agostino Rubini, Ruggiero Bascapé and Domenica Fontana; the presence of the three artists at the villa can be proven for 1st September 1581. While Alessandro Maganza's frescoes in the dome area still left the architectural structure relatively untouched, Ludovico Dorigny, between 1680 and 1687, decorated the walls below the balustrade in the style of lavish illusory Baroque. Other than in the decoration of the Villa Barbaro by Veronese, who strove to achieve a widening of the rooms, Dorigny altered the walls by painted architecture and sculptures apparently placed in front of the walls to create small sections and a diversity that is contrary to Andrea Palladio's architectural concept.

Imitators of the Villa Rotonda would each deserve a chapter to themselves, to deal with similarities and variations. Special attention should be called to at least one example: Mereworth Castle (Kent), built by Colin Campbell between 1722 and 1725.

The dome fresco in the great hall of the Villa Rotonda. The master who did these frescoes was Alessandro Maganza. The external structure of the dome can also be seen in the inside of the villa. The multiple layering of the dome appears to enclose the allegorical frescoes with several concentric circles. The lantern forms the central point, from which the frames of the frescoes recede in a star form.

pp. 200/201: the great hall of the Villa Rotonda. Palladio did not live to see the decoration of the hall by Ludovico Dorigny and a further unknown master. The frescoes, which by their illusionistic painting outplay and make unclear the harmonic proportions of the interior, would not be what he had in mind.

Villa Sarego

Santa Sofia di Pedemonte (Verona)

The rule of the Scalans, which included the area around Verona, was overthrown in 1387. The subsequent rule of the Viscontis over this area lasted only a short time, and in 1405 Verona submitted to the Republic of Venice. A property near Santa Sofia was given to the Sarego family at a time when the Scalans were still in power. In 1381, Antonio della Scala left a villa "with a dove-cote, well, wine-press and other equipment" to Cortesia Sarego. The region in which the Sarego's estate lay was very fertile, and in the following period the Sarego family showed that they knew how to make use of this.

One of Cortesia Sarego's descendants, Marcantonio Sarego, requested a plan for a new villa building on the estate near Santa Sofia of Palladio, nearly two hundred years after the gift was made. This was not the only offer that the Sarego family made to Andrea Palladio. Contemporary sources tell us that they were also interested in the building of villas by Palladio in Miega, Veronella, Beccacietta and Cucca. Michelangelo Murraro sees the reason for hardly any of these projects being carried out in the Sarego family's demand that Palladio himself should supervise the building schemes, which would hardly have been possible in view of the way Palladio was overloaded with commissions. Nonetheless, one of the buildings he created for the Sarego family has come down to us in Santa Sofia near Verona, though it is only a fragment.

We are quite well informed about the activities of the Sarego family in the middle of the sixteenth century since their private archives were made available to research. Their activities extended over both political and agricultural fields. We even encounter one of their members as an ambassador of the Republic of Venice. This makes the fact that there is a total lack of documents relating to the building in Santa Sofia all the more remarkable. The assumption that Marcantonio Sarego considered a new building because of his marriage to Ginevra Alighieri in the time around 1550 is no more than supposition. A rough determining of the date of origin of the Villa Sarego would have to put it in the time between 1560 and 1570. This period of time can be further reduced if one is prepared to follow James Ackermann and infer from the gross divergences of the building (even though only a fragment was

p. 203: ground-plan and view of the Villa Sarego from the Quattro Libri. The Saregos were an influential noble family in the area around Verona. Their requirements from the building that Palladio was to design were in accordance with this fact. Palladio sketched an estate of imposing greatness for the Saregos, which clearly took its bearings from Roman tradition.

pp. 204/205: view of the courtyard in the Villa Sarego. Restoration work on the building was carried out in the nineteenth century, and this could hide the fact that in this building we are dealing with a fragment. Only a small part of the planned building was carried out. The pictured courtyard view corresponds only to the left part of the inner courtyard in the sketch.

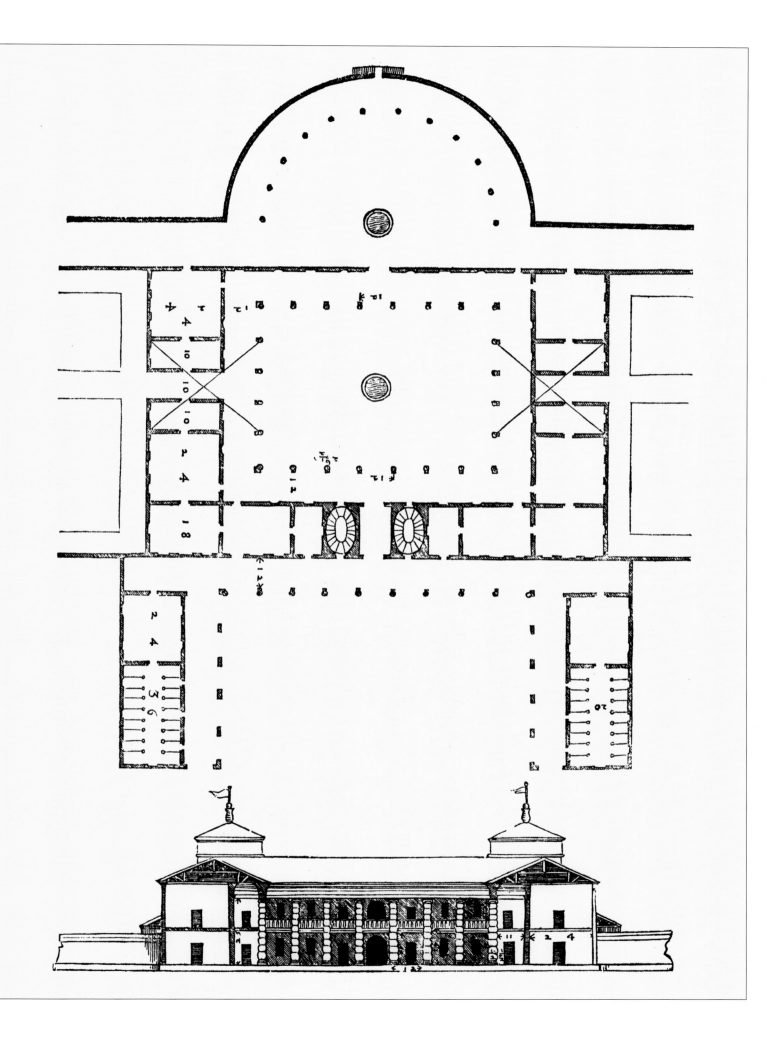

built) from the plan published in the *Quattro Libri* that the architect, who absolutely wanted to include the plan in his treatise, was over-precipitate. Such an assumption would fix the start of the construction work at some time around 1569. According to Marcantonio Sarego's will, an inhabitable building must already have existed in 1572. In addition, in 1570 Palladio seemed very confident that his plan would be carried out completely, for in his architectural treatise the Villa Sarego is described as already being a completed building.

This plan of Palladio's is fairly unusual in the framework of his creative work, though. Whether ambitions of the client to make his intentions of power manifest through architecture played a part in Palladio's plan must be left open to question. That the entire lay-out, however, would have, due to its massive appearance, in no way merged to a unity with the surrounding landscape had it been completed, but would rather have had the appearance of a fortress, should not be overlooked. The assumption that Palladio wanted to make a reference to the markedly military traditions of the Veronese in his plan could be a reason for the unusual actions of the architect.

While the assumption of such a reference to tradition must remain speculation, the adoption of another tradition is quite clearly recognisable. Palladio himself makes the decisive allusion in the description of the villa in his *Quattro Libri*. In the same breath as praising the charm

Above: the colossal columns of the inner courtyard have been executed in a rough rustication. Palladio thereby took up stylistic elements, which on the one hand were often used in Verona, but on the other also moved the Villa Sarego closer to Mannerist architecture.

206

Right: two sculptures made out of beric limestone stand surrounded by semi-circular hedges in front of the Villa Sarego. Due to the delicate composition of their main sides and their slender shapes – here evidently a representation of Diana – they make a somewhat lost impression against the massive building fragment.

and beauty of the estate, he reports that this place was appreciated in Roman times. When we recall that the memory of later Roman architecture was kept especially vivid in Verona by the buildings of Sanmicheli, such a statement can be regarded as a further ennobling of the estate. It can hardly be doubted that, in his design of the Villa Sarego, Palladio was once again dealing with "Roman residences", an ideal type which can be traced back to his studies of Vitruvius.

How then should one imagine a completed Villa Sarego? Any visitor would first have stepped into a courtyard, which would have been bordered both to left and right by the farming wings. Whether these farming wings, which were evidently meant to have round arch arrangements placed in front of them, were meant to be built with two storeys in correspondence with the mansion house, is something we

can only guess at. In his description, Palladio merely talks of roofed buildings on each side of the courtyard, "which serve for whatever work arises in a villa". The front of the mansion would have appeared in commanding majesty in the eyes of the visitor. A two-storeyed loggia with a colossal column order was intended. Pilasters placed behind these columns on the ground floor would have taken on the weight of the upper loggia. The wings, which the Sarego family would have lived in, would have lain at right angles around a courtyard, without enclosing it completely. The side opposite the entrance would have been closed off by a wall, which would still have given entrance to the semi-circular garden that lay beyond it. An encircling peristyle, whose columns would have been of the colossal order, was intended for this courtyard. As in the front courtyard, pilasters would have been placed behind the columns, which would have had to bear the weight of the upper loggia.

In this courtyard Palladio appears to fuse two elements of Roman residences as reconstructed from the writings of Vitruvius and Leon Battista Alberti: the atrium and the peristyle courtyard. The surface area of this courtyard was evidently, in accordance with Palladio's requirements, intended as the base of an atrium. In order to establish the length of such an atrium, he writes, one has first to form a square, whose side lengths are set by the width of the atrium; the diagonal of this square gives the measurement for the length of the atrium. It is precisely this principle that evidently forms the basis of the design of the ground-plan for the inner courtyard of the Villa Sarego. Of Palladio's plan, it is the left half of the mansion with its loggias that was carried out.

Whether the lay-out of a courtyard with an encircling peristyle can be seen as successful in connection with the colossal column order, can justly be questioned. It is vital not to be distracted by the present condition of the Villa Sarego: in 1857 restoration work was performed, the result of which is able to give the impression that one is dealing not with a fragment but with a completed building. What we see today is only half of the planned courtyard. But let us imagine this courtyard with the effect it would have had if completed. The massive colossal columns would have released a power far beyond the space provided by the courtyard. In addition, the vertical power of the columns is nowhere slowed down or diverted onto the horizontal line. An opportunity to balance the forces would have been offered by the balustrade of the upper loggia. But it is not taken. Because it is slightly recessed, its effect is less that of an encircling balustrade than that of one composed of segments and set up between the columns. So while on the one hand we can assume an ingenious fusion of atrium and columned courtyard, it is on the other hand opposed by a visual impression which, by the disproportion of the structural means, moves the courtyard close to Mannerist architecture. This imbalance has already been referred to in research, and Erik Forssmann writes that it would reflect too slavish an admiration of Palladio, if one were rashly to call this device beautiful or even merely adequate.

If one starts with the proposed date of origin of about 1569, then the Villa Sarego is Palladio's last villa project. Once more, in his late phase, he remembers his debt to Ancient Rome.

San Francesco della Vigna

Campo di San Francesco della Vigna (Venice)

Palladio's work on the church of San Francesco della Vigna in Venice was limited to the shaping of the façade. Jacopo Sansovino had supplied a model for the church as early as 1534, which was carried out with alterations as a long hall with side chapels.

After 1562, Palladio was commissioned to carry out the façade according to his own design. The precise date of origin is unknown, but it should be possible to deduce it approximately from Palladio's artistic development: on the one hand it represents a "draft" of the façade of San Giorgio Maggiore, which was presumably planned in 1565, but on the other hand does not yet achieve the unity of the show side of Il Redentore, in which its greater proximity to San Giorgio becomes apparent. So a date of about 1570 is likely.

Palladio took the inside of the church into consideration only insofar as he allowed the arrangement of the hall and connected chapels to be recognisable in the vertical division into three parts. As in San Giorgio, he rejects the horizontal subdivision into two storeys that was the custom in Venetian tradition. On the other hand, a colossal column order with an Attic storey and triangular gable dominates the central part, and here also the structures in front of the walls, which are three-quarter columns, seem to protrude from the surface of the wall in an almost freely plastic fashion. Nevertheless, the impression of a free-standing portico with a wall immediately behind it does not become apparent. The small columns, which flank the portal, and their projecting entablature bring about a fusion of the colossal order and the façade wall.

The side parts of the façade are also more closely connected with the centre by the general relationship of their outline. A uniformly stepped base develops along the entire width of the façade which, although it juts out more strongly in the middle, offers the same height to all its structural elements. Above all, however, it is the side axes that receive a structural motif closely related to the central part. While framing pilasters determine the outer end walls of the side aisles in San Giorgio, in San Francesco it is likewise the areas which project from the wall in the shape of three-quarter columns that are, in connection with the half gables, directly related to the dominating centre.

Above: the second Franciscan church in Venice got its name from the vineyard (la vigna) which the influential Ziani family had given to the order as land for building in 1232. We know nothing about the appearance of the first church.

p. 211: the beginning of the planning of this church dates right back to the time of the Doge Andreas Gritti. Jacopo Sansovino was meant to be commissioned with the design of the church building. The design and completion of the church façade can be attributed to Andrea Palladio.

Palazzo Barbarano
Contrada Porti 11 (Vicenza)

When Andrea Palladio was commissioned by Montano Barbaro to build a town palace for him, the piece of land that he was to build on confronted him with a serious problem: like many of his town palaces, the Palazzo Barbarano also had to stretch backwards. As two other built-on properties cut into Marcanton Barbarano's property on the left side, Palladio did not have a regular rectangle at his disposal. As he was understanding more and more how to make his spatial arrangement dynamic, this will have annoyed him considerably, as he was robbed of the opportunity to conceive a spatial axis determined by a tightening followed by a separation (as in the Palazzo Valmarana). In addition, he had to take the Via di Riale into consideration, whose slanting course meant that the right side façade of the palace to be built would meet the main façade at an obtuse angle.

The plan which Palladio produced despite the awkward conditions and published in the *Quattro Libri* offered only a faint echo of the differentiated and exceedingly dynamic system of tightening and the following opening which he had developed for the ground-plan of the Palazzo Valmarana. Even though the plan intended a central axis with an uninterrupted course, the shape of the property prevented its being made dynamic, as a symmetrical relationship of the two rows of rooms to each other could not be achieved.

Building was started in 1570, and a large part of the right wing of the palace must have been completed quite soon – Montano Barbarano then bought the two properties that encroached on it and asked Palladio to use them henceforth in the structure, without however tearing anything down of the part of the palace that had already been built. Consequently, Palladio's ground-plan design which he had managed to produce in his conflict with the unfortunate circumstances of the property had completely failed. Herbert Pée has rightfully denied the claim to artistic validity of the plan as it was now carried out; the end result, given the circumstances, makes a more than precipitate impression in its disorganised and asymmetrical arrangement.

The main façade can however count as an artistic achievement of high standing, even though the disruption of the entire plan, which

"No work of art is absolute, even if it is produced by the greatest and most practised artist: however much he might make himself the master of the material with which he is working, he still cannot alter its nature. So he can only produce in a certain sense and certain conditions that which he has in mind, and that artist whose powers of invention and imagination as it were connect directly with the material with which he has to work, will always be the most excellent one. This is one of the great excellences of ancient art: and just as people can only then be called clever and fortunate, when they live in the greatest freedom with the limitations of their nature and circumstances, so those artists deserve our greatest admiration, who wanted to do no more than their material permitted them to, and nevertheless did so much with it, that we are scarecely able to recognise their merit, even if we exert and train our mental faculties."
(Johann Wolfgang Goethe, Material of the Fine Arts, October 1786)

could no longer be corrected, can be seen there also. The construction work must already have progressed so far, that the portal had already been fixed into the wall. As no part of the building that had already been built could be torn down, the portal that really belongs in the centre of the façade appears to be forced to the right side of the façade. Despite this flaw in its beauty, the façade of the Palazzo Barbarano is extremely richly devorated.

In the *Quattro Libri*, Palladio suggests two possibilities for the treatment of the façade: the use of a composite colossal column order and the placing, one over the other, of an Ionic column arrangement in the base storey and a Corinthian column arrangement in the piano nobile. Probably because the façade had to border a narrow street, they decided in favour of the second solution, as a colossal column order would have made an overwhelming impression in the narrow street. The bases of the columns stand at ground level and spread beyond a three-part base storey. This starts with a smooth base, which ends at a projecting ledge, which at the same time serves as the lower ledge of the windows. The window frames are formed out of narrow pilasters, on whose capitals rests a projecting mezzanine area. The intercolumniation of the base storey above the smooth base is done in stone cut smoothly and distinctively. There are no corresponding windows cut into the mezzanine area; instead, reliefs with figures were set in it. As the palace was originally meant to be seven axes wide, only six reliefs were produced in correspondence with this first plan. There are, though, openings over the two outer windows on the left side of the base storey, which inform us that decorative reliefs were meant to be fixed there too. The base storey is closed off by an Ionic entablature which is richly decorated with stucco garlands. The piano nobile above it stands out, in contrast to the relative strictness of the smooth cut stone in the base storey, due to its rich ornamental decorations.

View of the Palazzo Barbarano from the Quattro Libri. In a further drawing of the view of the façade, Palladio dispensed with the colossal order of the columns, an idea which also corresponds to the completed building.

Right: Palazzo Barbarano. Façade. The two-storey order underlines the vertical alignment of the palace. The palace façade has an asymmetrical appearance, as the building was, in the course of a later expansion of the property, widened by two axes.

p. 214: Palazzo Barbarano. Detail of a window in the lower storey. Reliefs like the one produced here were meant to be set above all the windows of the lower storey. Such reliefs are, however, missing from over two windows. Evidently the reliefs were already made at the start of the construction work on the palace, because only six reliefs were originally required.

Alternately closed off by triangular and segmental arch gables, the windows of the piano nobile have strongly projecting balusters underneath them. Two sculptures rest on each of the window gables and fill in the surface between the gables and the Corinthian entablature, while stucco garlands which hang down between the columns and the window profiles break the rest of the wall surface up.

The overall effect is to present a façade which in both the turbulent rhythm of the column arrangements and the extremely differentiated layering backwards due to the extraordinarily rich ornamentation divests the façade of its traditional function as the end of the building, in that the situation of the walls is made totally unclear. The plasticity of the façade is heightened further by the light and by the narrowness of the street, and presents it less as a function of the Palazzo Barbarano than of the street that it borders.

Loggia del Capitaniato

Piazza dei Signori (Vicenza)

The Loggia del Capitaniato, which lies opposite the main façade of the basilica on the Piazza dei Signori, is the most impressive and characteristic example of a stately town building in Palladio's late work. Four colossal three-quarter columns rise from pedestals that are worked from white cut stone. Their dynamic rise is continued in the high capitals, which are composite (formed from the fusion of the Corinthian and Ionic orders). The vertical flow of movement is taken up by the way the entablature and surrounding balustrade are offset and ends with the flat pilasters of the closing half-storey. However meaningful the colour change between white cut stone and red brick is for the entire effect, the impression of a work carried out mainly in small brickwork hardly arises: the monumental nature of the design triumphs, as in other Palladian works, over the material.

The strong relief of the main façade, which is already somewhat qualified by the apparent severing of the columns from the wall, is heightened by the projecting balconies in front of the windows of the piano nobile and by the powerfully protruding ledge of the balustrade. Light and shadow combine with the two tones of the colourful material. The rich stucco decorations on the remaining wall surfaces, which were presumably created at the workshop of Lorenzo Rubini, who frequently worked together with Palladio, do not obscure the overall architectural structure. They have the effect of decorations that have been applied at a later date, rather than as a constituent part of the building.

The structure of the side wall, which faces the Via del Monte, is a surprising contrast to the façade. In a relationship to the serlian motif, an arcade arrangement opens here between what are, however, two closed wall surfaces in front of which there stand larger-than-life figures on high bases. Other than at the façade, the wall here has a horizontal structure: the motif of the balconies, which on the main side are limited to the width of the windows in the piano nobile, and from which the entire height dominates the clearly uniting vertical lines of the three-quarter columns, is here added as a dominant structural motif between the two stories. The wall of the piano nobile appears to be positively overrun with richly figurative stucco decorations, whose

"At the Loggia del Delegato (del Capitaniato, author), opposite the basilica, Palladio unjustly used his great forms for a small task; the early Renaissance managed to do such things better. The side façade, where he made the columns only as high as the ground floor and treated the whole in a more decorative manner, suggests that he had recognised his mistake."
(Jacob Burckhardt, The Cicerone, 1855)

216

programme glorifies the victory of the Venetians over the Turks in the Battle of Lepanto in 1571.

Despite plentiful documentary records, there are a number of unsolved questions with regard both to the past history and the construction of the existing building. We know that a building with a large columned hall was built at the beginning of the fifteenth century, which it was decided should be the residence of the Venetian governor in 1404. The appearance of this building cannot be definitely reconstructed from old town views of Vicenza. As late as 1521, Titian and Paris Bordone were commissioned to decorate the façade with frescoes. On 31st January 1565 there followed a decision of the town council to buy up and tear down all the houses and workshops between the loggia and the Contra dei Gudei, in order to build a further splendid loggia there and to erect a hall for the town council over it. This resolution does not however appear to have been followed by any kind of action.

Documents do not describe the condition of the old loggia as dilapidated until 18th April 1571.

After an evidently lively discussion about the question of whether to restore the old building or build a new one, the decision went in favour of a completely new project. The work on the building progressed only slowly.

There can be no doubts about the authorship of Palladio, as the

The Loggia del Capitaniato is regularly covered with decorative elements. The stucco-work was put on to the stone work. Much of this small work has now fallen off, so that the bare stonework is revealed in the spaces between the columns.

inscription between the left balcony on the façade gives his name: "Andrea Palladio i(nventore) archit(ecto)." As he himself oversaw the construction, it can scarcely be supposed that he was strongly tied to Venice by his commitments in the 1570s.

But further questions remain. Should we assume a change of plan between the façade and the side facing the Via del Monte? This idea is suggested by the extremely different structure. But neither of the two concepts can have come into existence before 1571: the allegories of the Battle of Lepanto on the side face rule out the possibility of its having been planned before 1571. But a planning date before 1571 can equally be excluded as a possibility for the façade, which faces on to the Piazza dei Signori: would Palladio otherwise have failed to mention a building of such impressive quality in his *Quattro Libri*, which appeared in 1570? So we must in all likelihood start with the assumption that the existing Loggia del Capitaniato was carried out according to a uniform plan.

The second question is: is the building that was built after 1571 a complete whole or only part of what was originally intended to be a larger building? The past history of the Loggia – whether as the residence of the Venetian governor or as a meeting place for the Vicenzan town council – would tend to suggest a building of greater size. Considerations as to the situation regarding urban development point in the same direction: although it is obviously a sort of counterpart to the basilica, the Loggia dei Capitaniato in no way takes that building's alignment into consideration.

For these reasons it has been supposed that five or even seven axes were originally thought of. As there are no documents about the design or definite written pieces of information, neither one nor the other thesis can be proved. The Museo Civico in Vicenza owns a sketch of a villa which is attributed to Palladio, and which is sometimes considered to be an early rough sketch of the building, that was started on in 1571. This drawing cannot be formally connected with the present Loggia del Capitaniato, though. A wide flight of steps leads up to a five-axis arch arrangement, which is flanked by fluted half-columns. An entablature, which is shaped in various ways and divides the two storeys firmly without being offset, is situated above the area of the capitals, which is developed into a richly decorated horizontal value by means of arabesques over the arches. The relatively low upper storey opens between flat pilasters into upright rectangular areas. Figures stand on the lightly offset final ledge in front of a flat roof which is hipped at the sides. The supposition that the façade of the Loggia del Capitaniato previously stretched to five axes is justified in principle insofar as two further column arrangements on the left hand side would have brought the side wall precisely into line with the basilica.

For the present-day visitor, though, the Loggia del Capitaniato makes the impression, despite the varied structure of its façades, of a work that is a unified whole, and whose proportions of height and width it would be difficult to imagine altered. As it is placed immediately opposite the main side of the basilica, we have a fine illustration of Palladio's development from the stage of his first mastery to his later

Above and p. 221: on the façade of the Loggia del Capitaniato, Andrea Palladio elevated the supporting powers to a formal principle. The rising characteristic movement of the columns is made even stronger by the way the upper ledge is offset.

"And if the building is meant to be decorated with columns or pilasters, then the bases, capitals and architraves should be made out of natural stone, but the other parts out of burnt stone." (Andrea Palladio, 1570)

style. At the same time, a comparison is invited all the more as the two buildings are related to each other both in their situation in the town – their position on the large square – and in their function as buildings of town or state representation.

On these premises, the two buildings which are separated from each other in their dates of origin by about twenty years should be seen as opposite poles rather than as different points on a common line of development. While, at the basilica, the impression of something lying down predominates, at the Loggia del Capitaniato it is that of something upright. The thought suggests itself of holding the widely elongated building of the older Palazzo della Ragione responsible for the arrangement of the loggias on the basilica. But when one compares the two, one sees how very emphatically Palladio supports the horizontal directional values of the older work, while they are reduced on the Loggia del Capitaniato to small sections that do not merge into a continuum. Furthermore, in his later works Palladio counters the equal rights of juxtaposition and co-operation of the parts with the dominance of a single motif, to which the other elements are related, no matter how richly arranged they are. Not least, the multiply layered "relief" of the loggias on the basilica gives way to a positively baroque "modelling power". This becomes especially clear on the colossal columns, which no longer grow out of the wall as half-columns, but detach themselves from the surface as three-quarter columns that we could almost put our arms around.

The Loggia del Capitaniato is an example of Palladio's late style of town façades. The roots of this development can however be traced back to the preceding decades. Palladio had considered the idea of a colossal half-column order for the first time around 1550, when he was planning the courtyard of the Palazzo Iseppo Porto in Vicenza, but this idea was not implemented. At that time, though, he had not intended three-quarter, but half-columns, and horizontal stresses would have played a far greater part there than on the later Loggia. The shape of the three-quarter columns which detach from the wall appears for the first time on the façade of San Giorgio Maggiore in Venice, whose basic plan was probably made during the years around or shortly after 1565, despite its having been implemented later. Finally, the tendency towards standardization characterizes more or less all of Palladio's buildings after about 1565, with regard both to the walls and to the ground-plans.

While one may feel the strong dissection of the surfaces and the overdone decorative elements to be Mannerist, the overall impression nonetheless points to the future, and to consider the façade of the later Palazzo Porto-Breganze, which remained a fragment, will confirm this impression: the way forward to the Baroque now seems clear.

Palazzo Porto-Breganze

Piazza Castello (Vicenza)

This fragment of a palace façade that rises like a tower is not mentioned as one of Palladio's works until the eighteenth century. We lack any definite documents about the history of the building and planning. Vincenzo Scamozzi, whose *Idea dell'Architettura Universale* appeared in Venice in 1615, classified the palace amongst other completed façades of this type. Today Palladio is generally accepted as the author.

The date of the start of the construction and the reasons for breaking off the work are also unknown. The palace does not yet exist on a town view dating from 1571. If we assume that Palladio is the author, then it must have originated during the last years of Palladio's life.

Indeed, there is a close connection between it and the Loggia del Capitaniato in the extremely powerful and plastic detailed work of the two axes and in the dominance of vertical directional values. In contrast to the structure of the latter building, the columns which grow out of the wall in a three-quarter curve are placed on very high pedestals (one is reminded of the façade of San Giorgio Maggiore). The column bases start on a line with the tops of the windows.

In order to see the fragment with the right proportions, one has presumably to add five further axes to the façade. One of Francesco

View of the façade of the Palazzo Porto-Breganze according to Ottavio Bertotti-Scamozzi. In this drawing, Bertotti-Scamozzi reconstructs the palace according to the fragment, which Vicenzo Scamozzi had already changed by his interventions. In particular, the fruit branches between the capitals form an horizontal value in the reconstruction, which would have disturbed the vertical structure of the façade.

Right: The Palazzo-Breganze is also called the "Ca' del diavolo" – devil's house – in the vernacular. This expression probably harks back to the fact that there used to be a brothel nearby.

Muttoni's drawings gives us some clues about this: a further axis of the same sort adjoining on the left would have been followed by a central part distinguished by its slightly greater width, and the whole building would have to be imagined completed symmetrically by a further three axes. The façade would have achieved its full effect only in this multiple repetition and its full importance in the history of the development of architecture would then have become clear. Despite all the differences in individual forms, the high base under the shapes in front of the wall and the way the columns become independent from the wall and the building is offset above the capitals remind us of High Baroque palaces such as the Palais Czernin in the Hradčany in Prague, which was built between 1669–92 by the northern Italian architect Francesco Caratti.

Le Zitelle
Giudecca (Venice)

Situated between Il Redentore and the Isola di San Giorgio, this façade on the Canale di Giudecca adds a beautiful touch to that part of Venice. Its relationship to Palladio's work is just as unclear as its construction history. Records have come down to us that show that the Jesuits bought a property on the Giudecca in 1561, on which an institute "alla Presentazione della Vergine" for the education of impoverished girls was to be built. The church building, which was moreover altered later, was begun after 1580 according to the records and completed in 1586.

The gabled façade, which is divided strictly in two storeys by a flat

Below: Andrea Palladio is mentioned for the first time in the seventeenth century as being the architect of the church "Le Zitelle" in Venice. The church is associated with the institute "alla Presentazione della Vergine".

horizontal ledge consists of a framing arrangement of flat double pilasters. Only the portal, which is flanked by half-columns and ends with a gable that projects strongly from the wall, is emphatically plastic in character. The upper storey opens out with a wide thermal window. The silhouette of the entire buildings, with the small bell-towers over the façade and the dominating dome, reminds one of Palladio's last church, the Tempietto near the Villa Maser.

The church is not described as having been built according to a model of Palladio's until the beginning of the seventeenth century. A façade sketch after Palladio that A. Visentini has preserved shows a close connection to Le Zitelle, but probably represents an earlier stage in the planning. The windows in the lower storey are brought into harmonic accord with the gabled portal and the towers and dome are missing. Horizontal and vertical directional values are completely balanced. The completed building conflicts with this plan in various respects. It is therefore more than likely — if one is prepared to suppose that Visentini's drawing reproduces one of Palladio's plans — that the executing architect, Jacopo Bozzetto, revised this plan, which probably dates from the early 1560's. Such an assumption can of course not be advanced with certainty as long as we lack definite documents.

The building of the church of Le Zitelle was carried out to the greater part in the eighteenth century. But as its façade, despite stylistic inconsistencies, displays Palladian formal properties, we can nonetheless conjecture that Andrea Palladio was at the very least involved in the design of the façade.

"Seen from a socio-economical point of view, Venice at the time of its great economic rise had all the advantages and shortcomings of a modern city. Though most of the population crammed together in Venice had work . . ., differences in the degree of prosperity remained considerable. These differences were made all the more acute by a wave of consumerism . . . That wave had the effect of highlighting the standard of living of the poor even more, though; the poor were protected by a law passed in 1529 and aimed at regulating social welfare, but nevertheless hunger and the increases in the grain prices sometimes meant they were the victims of severe privation."
(Alvise Zorzi, 1985)

Teatro Olimpico

Piazza Matteotti (Vicenza)

Since the Olympian Society, of which Palladio was a founder member, was set up in Vicenza, they had made do with having plays performed in the House of the Academy, the "Casa academica", for the most part doing without stage equipment. In the 1570s, plans to build a theatre began to take concrete shape. In 1579, a piece of ground near the disused fortress was bought. The decision to carry out the building of the theatre was taken on 15th February 1580. Palladio was asked for plans and a model and it was already possible to start on the construction work on 20th February 1580. We unfortunately have no idea what the model looked like. Palladio's ideas are conveyed to us solely by a drawing of the stage façade, the "scenae frons".

The fact that the architect was evidently able to supply a plan within a very short space of time resulted from the examination he had been making of the task of designing a theatre for longer than two decades. His earliest treatment of the theme of the theatre building resulted in his attempt to produce a reconstruction of Vitruvius's theatre, which

Section through the Teatro Olimpico. Palladio was able to supply the design of the Teatro Olimpico in a relatively short time. The reason for this was that he had begun, twenty years before, to tackle the task of structuring a theatre. During this time, he attempted a reconstruction of the Vitruvian theatre along with Daniele Barbaro.

Palladio supplied as a wood engraving for Daniele Barbaro's edition of Vitruvius, published in 1556. It is based on sketches of ancient theatre ruins in Verona, Rome, Pola and Vicenza itself. In it the street perspectives, which appear in the arcades, are only sketched flatly. Palladio had already designed the stage fittings for the Academy's "ancient Olympic Games" in 1558. It was intended that Hercules, the founder of the Olympic Games, should be fêted. We do not have any pictorial representation of the ideas that Palladio developed within this context, and not even written evidence gives us a reasonably clear indication. Frescoes dating from the 1590's inform us roughly what an arrangement that was put up in 1561–62 in the hall of the Palazzo della Ragione, the so-called basilica, made out of wood, and probably soon destroyed, looked like. It appears to have anticipated certain essential features of the later Teatro Olimpico. Palladio finally, in 1564–65, put up a "half-theatre made of wood" in Venice for the Compagnia della Calza degli Accesi, which evidently stood in the cloisters of the convent of the Carità. Vasari notes that Palladio "built a wooden amphitheatre in the form of a colosseum for the gentlemen of the Compagnia della Calza".

Whether we are really dealing with a theatre built on an elliptical ground-plan and surrounded on all sides by rising seat rows modelled on the Colosseum or the Theatre of Marcellus in Rome must remain open to question. We can assume an exterior façade with many storeys.

At any rate, in 1580 Palladio was able to fall back on a wealth of previous considerations when planning the Teatro Olimpico. He planned an exceedingly richly structured wooden stage wall, whose three storeys would be differentiated from each other in various ways. The lower storey is presented in the form of the motif of a widened triumphal arch: free-standing columns backed by pilasters form three axes

Ground-plan of the Teatro Olimpico. The Olympian Society of Vicenza was influential in the award of the contract to plan a theatre. A large part of the plan must have been carried out by Palladio's death in 1580. The Olympian Society at first showed little appreciation of the street perspectives. The director Angelo Ingegneri advised that the planned street perspectives be added for the performance of the play Oedipus Rex.

pp. 228/229: the forming of the upper end of the auditorium took place in 1914. The solution probably largely complies with the original design, as the illusion of an open room is also striven for in other parts of the theatre.

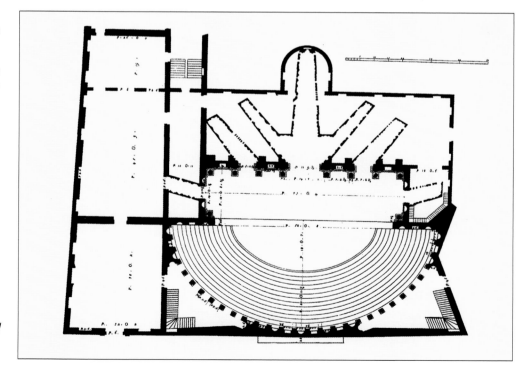

The illusion of an open space is also alluded to in the auditorium: it is surrounded by a colonnade, whose intercolumniation is partly open, as in this picture. The remaining spaces between the columns incorporate niches with statues.

on both left and right, the central one in each case being broken through by a rectangular door, while the side axes are taken up by tabernacle niches, with small columns and triangular gables. The centre of this "scenae frons" is formed by a wide round arch, also on free-standing columns, which projects considerably into the middle storey. The latter is somewhat lower and the amount of modelling is reduced. In the side axes, half-columns in front of pilasters flank three figure tabernacles of equal size, which are nonetheless given a rhythmical pattern: while the niches at the sides have segmental arch gables, the central one in each case has a triangular gable. The ledge over this middle storey repeats mainly the profiles of the entablature, but does this to a reduced extent in order to correspond with the reduction of the height of the storeys. A sort of Attic storey, which is once again reduced in its height and plastic modelling forms the upper end, and its axes are divided merely by pilasters, between which the wall areas no longer contain shadowy niches, but are meant for representational reliefs.

So there is a "diminuendo" in the dimensions and modelling of the

The "scenae frons" of the Teatro Olimpico: the stage wall, which is united despite its plentiful subdivision, is broken up by the rising floor level and the gradual narrowing of the street rows. Scenes from the life of Hercules are portrayed in the upper relief areas.

wall from the bottom to the top. The fact that, within this wealth of variation, all details both relate to each other and are connected to each other, is natural in view of previous works by Palladio. But Palladio had never combined horizontal and vertical directional values in such a differentiated and close network before.

The rich decoration of stucco sculptures had been included in the plan from the start, but was probably not of especial interest to Palladio. The statues in the niches represent members of the Academy in an ancient style of dress. Among others, Agostino Rubini, Ruggero Brascate and Domenico Fontana worked here as they did on other works by Palladio. The top Attic storey is decorated with reliefs of the Labours of Hercules, the patron of the Vicenzan Olympian Society, by Agostino Caneva.

The proscenium is delimited at the sides by wings that project at right angles towards the auditorium. They are shaped in imitation of the stage façade, but less lavishly since they are less visible.

On the other hand, the front of the stage and the auditorium are a lively contrast to each other. The steps of the auditorium rise around

231

the semi-circular "orchestra". This is bordered at the back by a column arrangement of the Corinthian order, the spaces between the columns being in part closed or open. Here too, the architect created a lively rhythm: three closed areas are followed by seven open ones, with nine closed ones in the centre, the pattern of seven and three continuing on the far side. Niches are set into the closed areas and have alternately curved and right-angled corners at their tops. Statues likewise made of stucco stand in them. The balustrade, which closes off the entire semi-circle at the back and above, is followed by a further sequence of stucco figures, which are meant to be a link up to the open sky. This poses the question as to what was originally planned as the upper conclusion of the auditorium. The present solution of a flat ceiling with a sky-blue colour and light clouds dates from 1914. But it probably comes close to the sixteenth century plans, as the intention was undoubtedly to create the illusion of a room without a roof, just as the colonnade which closes off the auditorium alludes to a position in the open.

Below left and right: the "scenae frons" of the Teatro Olimpico is richly decorated with statues placed in niches. A commitment of the members of the Olympian Society made in May 1580 intended each member to have a stucco statue made at his own cost, which would be put up in the niches of the building.

Palladio did not live to see the Teatro Olimpico completed. Although building evidently progressed rapidly at first, the completion of the entire building dragged on over many years. A deal was con-

cluded with Vincenzo Scamozzi on 6th May 1584, who then made a number of changes to the original project. He drew in the wings between the auditorium and the proscenium as a continuation of the colonnade at the back, so that the proscenium was by this changed into a self-contained stage area. Its independence is stressed by the not very original coffered ceiling. While Scamozzi, in this way, brought about a division of what Palladio presumably intended as the unity of the proscenium and auditorium, he also intervened emphatically in the overall effect of the stage façade. It was not until then, when further ground was bought, that the artistic street views with shortened perspectives were created behind the entrances to the "scenae frons". The rising floor level and gradual narrowing of the streets, which had a rich alternation of sham temples, palaces and houses, broke up the stage wall which was continuous despite its frequent subdivisions. In order to heighten this effect still further, Scamozzi evidently raised the height of the side entrances, over which Palladio had intended reliefs to be set, and also included the openings in the projecting side walls in this illusory room enlargement.

The theatre was officially opened in 1584 with a performance of Sophocles's tragedy *Oedipus Rex*.

The statues in the niches represent none other than the members of the Olympian Society personally. They appear in ancient costume in their niches. The need for fame of the founders and the obvious desire to set up a code of virtues as an iconographic programme, come together here.

Tempietto Barbaro

Maser (Treviso)

Towards the end of his life, Palladio received the opportunity to build a sacred centralised building: the Tempietto Barbaro in Maser. The connection of a "temple front" to a domed building refers to the Pantheon in Rome. In actual fact, though, two forms of centralised buildings fuse in the ground-plan: the circle and the Greek cross. The exterior of the building, which nowadays is cramped between garden walls, focuses entirely on the façade. A portico that is drawn out a long way, and has unusually steep proportions, leads along with the diagonal parts of the gable to two small bell-towers, which for their part pass on the upward-moving trend to the dome. The five spaces between the columns are framed by pillars, which are like the middle four columns in their entasis and tapering. The façade probably faced onto a small square originally.

"So we can read, that the ancients, when building their temples, endeavoured to pay attention to suitable decoration, which is the most beautiful part of architecture. And so we too, who do not have any such false idols, search out what is most perfect and excellent in order to satisfy the need for proper decoration where the temple form is concerned. And because this is the circular form, we make our temples round."
(Andrea Palladio, 1570)

The area inside has an alternation of deep niches on a rectangular ground-plan and closed wall areas with figure tabernacles between the eight regular half-columns. The lower part of the building is completed by an unbroken continuous ledge, whose profile – three flat bands which are contrasted with each other by ovolo moulding – is taken over from the arcade arches. An entablature, whose rich decoration with cherubs' heads and tendrils was presumably not in accordance with Palladio's wishes, forms the transition to the dome vault, along with a broken balustrade. The beginning of the dome is shifted slightly outwards and is therefore not visible – in continuation of the solution conceived for the dome over the crossways in San Giorgio Maggiore, the dome here appears to be hovering over the room, the incunabula of related solutions in late Baroque.

Though we are reminded of the Roman Pantheon, comparison will

Ground-plan and elevation of the Tempietto according to Bertotti-Scamozzi. "The round form is the most perfect and excellent form for places of worship . . .; because all its parts are after all at an equal distance from the centre, it is the most suitable to testify to the unity, the endless nature, the uniformity and the justice of God". (Andrea Palladio, 1570)

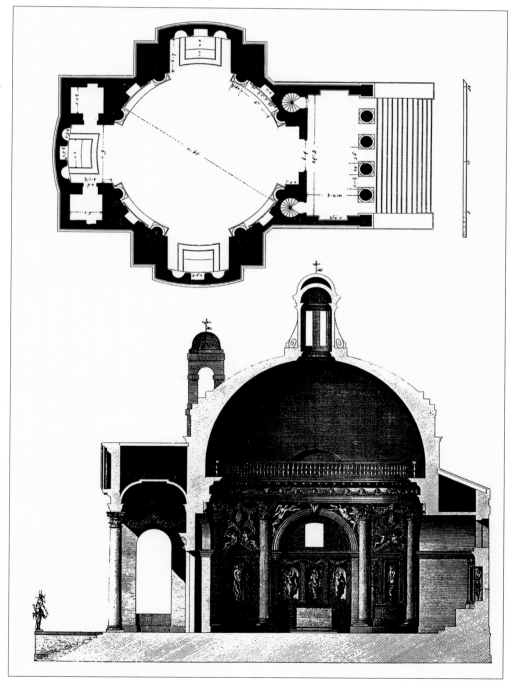

Right: the side with the entrance is clearly emphasized in the Tempietto Barbaro, which was conceived as a centralised building. A temple front is set in front of the main part of the building on this side. The entrance side is further emhasised by two small bell-towers.

p. 236: the Tempietto Barbaro was Andrea Palladio's last project. This sacred building was built, on the orders of Marcantonio Barbaro, immediately next to the Villa Barbaro in Maser.

make the differences clear. In the ancient building, the rising walls and vaulting appear as part of a unified spatial casing, even though it has richly arranged details. Palladio clearly contrasts the two forms of cylinder and semi-sphere in his late work by a repeated emphasis on horizontals, and, over and above that, divides them into a palpable terrestrial zone and into a light, celestial one that cannot be precisely gauged with the eye.

The overabundant stucco decorations that are of the type that the sculptor Alessandro Vittoria produced cannot have been in line with Palladio's intentions. One might well describe the final appearance in T. S. Ackermann's words: "This irreverent child of the Pantheon has more in common with the Rococo than with Roman architecture."

237

Palladio's Legacy

Palladio, by his own comments, directed every approach at an interpretation towards the exemplary pre-eminence of the ancients – or at least suggested antiquity as the only adequate measure for the judgement of his own works. But no master develops independently of the environment in which he grows up. Accordingly, the roots of Palladio's developing style can be traced to the context of the contemporary or immediately preceding architecture of the time. In his early villa buildings such as the Villa Godi in Lonedo, Palladio not only continued the type of two-towered villa, which was distinctive of Venetia, but in the rhythmical ordering of closed wall surfaces and openings fell back on the examples of his teachers' generation. The plastic subdivision of the wall came second to the dominance of the surface.

In the following years Palladio switched around the relationship between the sides and the middle part of the building: it is no longer the corner risalitos that protrude, but the central axis, which, furthermore, is distinguished by a gable. At the same time, the central part can either open up in the form of the so-called serlian motif (Villa Forni-Cerato in Montecchio Precalcino) or in three symmetrical round arch arrangements (Villa Gazzotti-Grimani in Bertésina). For the first time a tendency to emphasize volume and to centralize becomes apparent. Not until 1552, in the Villa Pisani in Montagnana, and one year later in the Villa Cornaro in Piombino Dese, did Palladio choose a two-storeyed portico to emphasize the central part of the building, and in 1554 he chose as his dominating motif in the Villa Chiericati in Vancimuglio a colossal column order under a gable, like the front of a temple. The impressions which his studies in Rome left him with are unmistakeable both in the whole and in the fashioning of detail, but on the other hand we should not forget that as early as 1472 Leone Battista Alberti had intended a gabled column order for the church of San Sebastiano in Mantua, and that Giuliano da Sangallo, in the 1480s, had integrated a five-axis column arrangement with a crowning gable into the façade of the Villa Poggio a Caiano near Florence.

Any attempt to track down in Palladio's work either an invariable constant or an unchanging direction in his development must fail. First

Title page copper engraving from Andrea Palladio's I Quattro Libri dell' Architettura, which was published in 1570 in Venice. Two English translations were published in London in the first half of the 18th century.

of all, Palladio's artistic temperament was too versatile (Goethe referred to his versatility) and he was forever adopting new ideas. Secondly, he reacted extremely sensitively to the conditions which were made by the clients regarding the function of a building and its position.

Palladio presumably received his first commission for the building of a town palace in about 1542. This was the Palazzo Thiene in Vicenza. In this early phase Palladio already demonstrated his ability to adapt himself to the needs and demands of his clients. His examination of the architecture of his time should not be ignored in this context. In particular, he was not able to hide his sympathy for the formal material of Giulio Romano. Nonetheless, he goes beyond a simple taking over of motifs – for example the window surrounded by consoles – and uses this motif by enclosing the consoles with columns in order to strengthen his own architectural statement.

Palladio reached the highpoint of his work with the loggias for the Palazzo della Ragione in Vicenza, the so-called Basilica. The Basilica, which along with the Villa Rotonda and the church of Il Redentore was the work that was emulated most frequently, offers us a yardstick to assess Palladio's relationship with Ancient Rome. The use of individual forms that imitate the placing one above the other of regularly shaped arch arrangements reminds us of Ancient Roman theatres such as the Colosseum or the Theatre of Marcellus is just as correct as the observation that the Ionic column order of the lower. But are such comments not too superficial? These ancient stylistic details had at that time long been a common property of Italian architecture, his recourse to column orders that change with each storey had already been found for a long time in both the sacred (Santa Maria dele Carceri in Prato, built by Giuliano da Sangallo between 1484 and 1495) and the secular areas (the courtyard of the Palazzo Farnese in Rome built by Giuliano da Sangello the Younger before 1546). What seems to be of importance here is the reference to the northern Italian tradition: the motif of two-storeyed loggias can for example be found in the Palazzo della Ragione in Padua. Built between 1420 and 1435, it is true that an arch arrangement in the ground storey corresponds to a double arch in the upper storey, but the motif is given – and more than that: here already are found the oculi in the spandrels of the arch arrangements. There can be no doubt that Palladio took this motif over from Padua. More important as a reference point is the library on St. Mark's Square in Venice that Jacopo Sansovino began in 1532: it is true that Sansovino differentiated the loggia of the ground floor and the sequence of windows of the upper storey, but he offers us the early stage of that form, which afterwards came to be known as the Palladio motif. In each of the window axes, a serliana is indicated which is however, contrary to tradition, projected into space, that is into the third dimension, by means of placing two columns in each case one behind the other. Against the background of such models, Palladio's own creative achievement becomes all the more apparent: by this regular shaping of upper and lower storeys he created a higher measure of unity, and by widening the horizontal closed intercolumniation into genuine openings, he created a shell for the space, which itself is permeated by

"I arrived here a few hours ago, have already been through the town and have seen the Olympian Theatre and Palladio's buildings. They have produced a most charming little book with copper engravings and a text that has artistic sense for the convenience of strangers. It is only when one sees the works in front of one that their true value becomes recognisable: for they are meant to fill the eye with their real size and corporeality and satisfy the mind with the lovely harmony of their dimensions, not only in the abstract sketches but with their entire perspective advancing and receding; and so I say about Palladio: he was rather an inward, and from his heart, a great person."
(Johann Wolfgang von Goethe, 19th September 1786 in Vicenza)

"No other architect of the sixteenth century showed antiquity such a fiery devotion as he, and no other penetrated so far into the deepest being of ancient monuments and was yet able to reproduce them so freely. He is almost the only one never to have kept to a single decorative effect, but organized himself exclusively according to the arrangement and the feeling for the relationships in his buildings."
(Jacob Burckhardt, The Cicerone, 1855)

space, as it were filled by space. External and internal space along with the structured wall constitute parts of a common whole.

What remains, beyond the adoption of individual forms from ancient Roman architecture, of the exemplary status of Palladio's so greatly praised antiquity? It is that inherent regularity, which is independent of individual formal loans in each of Palladio's works, which his so highly respected Vitruvius referred to more or less as follows: that in a good building, every part must be in just as harmonic an agreement with its neighbouring part as with the whole. In this all-embracing principle, Palladio felt himself to be related to the ancients, in his loyalty to this principle we see the single constant running through his entire work.

In this regularity Palladio also differs from his models. By dispensing with any decorative additions, he shaped both the storeys and the sequence of arch arrangements in total harmony. Horizontal and vertical lines were kept in complete symmetry, the ledge between the storeys having both a clearly dividing and, by means of the shoulder-piece, a connecting function contrary to such buildings as Sansovino's Venetian library.

The Palazzo Iseppo Porto harks back to antiquity once again. In this building, which was probably begun around 1549/50, Palladio was trying to revive the spatial sense of the Ancients (he refers specifically to the Greeks in his treatise). This applies both to the conception of the peristyle courtyard and to the strict separation of the living quarters of the master of the house from the guest accommodation.

By contrast, the façade of the Palazzo Iseppo Porto is wholly of Palladio's own time. The ground floor and the piano nobile are clearly marked off, a division which is underlined by the rustication of the lower storey and one which highlights the different degrees of importance of the two floors.

But in the buildings he designed in his mature and late periods, Palladio inclined to unification of the impact made by a façade, by emphasizing verticals and replacing the Mannerist subdivision of wall surfaces with a concept of unity. We see this elsewhere too; the Villa Barbaro in Maser, sketches for which were done in 1557/58, accentuates the main building by a colossal column order which presents itself to one's view head-on. Further examples to be mentioned include: the façade of the church of San Giorgio Maggiore in Venice, the Palazzo Valmarana in Vicenza that was planned in 1565, and then in sundry different forms the later works such as the Loggia del Capitaniato and the Palazzo Porto-Breganze in Vicenza, the Villa Sarego in Santa Sofia di Pedemonte and the façade of the church of Il Redentore in Venice.

In 1560 Palladio managed for the first time to gain a foothold in Venice, in the field of convent and of church building. The completion of the cloisters of Santa Maria della Carità (1560–1561) and the refectory of San Giorgio Maggiore (1560–1562) as well as the design of the façade of San Francesco della Vigna (after 1562) were followed in 1565 by the commission to complete the Benedictine church San Giorgio Maggiore, and in 1576–77, as the crowning of his activity in the field of church building, the planning of the votive church Il Redentore. That Palladio, whose architectural ideas stood in opposition to Venetian tradition, was now considered for the most stately tasks in the centre of the Republic, should not only be ascribed to his friendly relations with the Venetian patricians. Indeed, after the middle of the sixteenth century in northern Italy, he did not have any serious competition in either an artistic or technical respect. The traditional pattern of the cruciform domed church had peaked in the subtlety of buildings such as the San Salvatore in Venice (1507–34, presumably carried out according to sketches by Tullio Lombardi and in consultation with Jacopo Sansovino) and Santa Giustina in Padua (begun in 1532 by Andrea Moroni). The Republic's advisory architect, Jacopo Sansovino, could no longer contribute any innovative ideas as early as 1553, at the beginning of the new building work for the church of San Guliano in Venice: what resulted was a simple hall with three chapels next to the presbytery. Palladio would not have been chosen only with respect to his universally established reputation, but also on the basis of the particular requirements: in the cases of both San Giorgio Maggiore and Il Redentore, the requirements of town development had to be considered to a great extent. The façades had to establish an optical counterpoint to the Piazetta of San Marco over the Bacino di San Marco and the Canale della Guidecca. And no other architect of his time was by reason of his consideration of landscape or urban development and his allowance for an observer's distant and variable viewpoint predestined for this task to an equal degree as Palladio.

Palladio managed his tasks with the supreme ease of a specialist with the manifest experience of many years. Although the two great churches are entirely different in type – San Giorgio Maggiore follows the scheme of a three-aisled, cruciform basilica, Il Redentore the principle of a great hall closed off to the east – they represent closely related formal characteristics: in both cases Palladio strives for a unified well-lit space, in both former and latter the wall is experienced as the summation of plastically strong developed single elements, and in both buildings Palladio tries to get a fusion of the longitudinal and central buildings. Moreover, Il Redentore can be seen as the more highly differentiated form of San Giorgio Maggiore.

Notwithstanding the so different conditions of situation, function and the material facilities of the respective clients, questions arise with regard to Palladio's works concerning both artistic constants and stylistic development. The constant has already been referred to: it lies in the unfailing feeling for measure, legitimacy and order that connects Palladio with antiquity and which he admired in that antiquity. At the same time, however, a path of astonishing evolutionary range cannot be ignored which leads from his early works to his later years. Palladio strove primarily, from decade to decade, towards a higher measure of unity. If at first the whole appears as the sum of its parts, that is, as a kind of "concatenation", Palladio did however increasingly evolve a concept of the whole in which details were assigned their immovable place. In his façades and courtyards, and not least in his church

"I have found much that is reprehensible alongside the most exquisite details in the works that Palladio carried out, especially the churches. And when I considered how far I was being just or unjust to such an extraordinary man, it was as if he stood next to me and said: I did this and that against my will, because under the circumstances I could come close to my highest idea only in this way."
(Johann Wolfgang von Goethe, 6th October 1786 in Venice)

"In his church buildings, Palladio was – at least as far as the façades are concerned – a great innovator in comparison with what was up to then a Venetian system made up of many parts, which even Jacopo Sansovino had adapted himself to . . . The strict simplicity of the details, the constant calculation of the parts towards a whole, always produces a compelling impression in his works."
(Jacob Burckhardt, The Cicerone, 1855)

buildings, Palladio attained this unity first and foremost through a concentration in a vertical direction, around which the side rooms were symmetrically grouped, even though economic conditions often hindered the completion of these ideas. At the same time, the decorative elements which were used from the beginning only sparingly by Palladio in favour of the pure appearance of architecture diminished increasingly in importance. Where they were used in abundance in Palladio's late work – such as the façades of the Palazzo Barbarano or the Loggia del Capitaniato – they were merely applied, added on to the surfaces later, but had never developed from the structure of the building.

Finally, in the four decades in which we can follow Palladio's work, there increasingly appeared a tendency towards modelled shaping of façades and rooms, which in his later period led up to the beginning of a rising and falling modelling of surfaces. In this respect, Andrea Palladio has a forward-looking importance similar to Michelangelo with his work on St. Peter's in Rome.

Aside from the constants and variables in Palladio's work, there arises the problem of the historical classification of his style. As a "classicist" who is supposed to have taken his bearings mainly from ancient Roman architecture, he would most likely be classified as a descendant of the High Renaissance. Indeed he continued the High Renaissance in various respects. What points to this is the constantly renewed examination of the idea of the "pure" centralised building, which he was certainly able to realise at least twice in the Villa Rotonda and the Tempietto near the Villa Barbaro. Concentrating the spatial focus on a dominating dome in both of his great churches can be understood as the heritage of the High Renaissance, as can his admiration for Michelangelo, provided that we can include him in what Heinrich Wölfflin called the "classical art" of the post-classical stylistic epochs. Finally, it is the harmony of the parts which in each case are clearly related to each other or to the concept as a whole which seems to remove Palladio's work from any classification into his own epoch, which nowadays is generally termed Mannerism.

On the other hand, the very phenomenon of Palladio proves how enigmatic the term Mannerism is.

For however much Palladio's work can be derived from the epoch of the High Renaissance, he equally proves himself in individual details to be anti-classical in the manner of the sixteenth century. A careful examination of his works makes this clear many times: for instance, the infiltrating of a wall with space such as was "invented" for the basilica in Vicenza, cannot be explained either in the requirements of antiquity or those of the High Renaissance. The realisation of the "ideal" centralised building by at the same time turning around this thought – first of all concentrating the room towards the centre and then the use exclusively of centrifugal forces pushing outwards – such as characterises the Villa Rotonda, can be seen as a basic principle of Mannerist art: the interpretation of a "classical" model by anti-classical means. In a related manner the Villa Rotonda offers the synthesis of a further contradiction: the completely regularly developed and shaped model of a cube with four column porticos, so to speak an abstract, fuses in an unsurpassed manner with the preconditions of the surrounding landscape: abstract and concrete, rational and emotional factors all combine with each other. Furthermore: the column arrangements, which in San Giorgio Maggiore and in Il Redentore separate the presbytery from the monks' choir, allows one to look from the nave into an area whose length cannot be gauged by the eye. With all due care, one is reminded of the apparently infinitely long perspectives in the paintings of the same time, such as those of Jacopo Tintoretto.

The proofs that Palladio was a Mannerist night easily be prolonged endlessly. But at the same time, we must take into account the shortcomings that are of necessity connected with all generalizations in labelling our stylistic epochs. For the removal of clearly defined borders to rooms, the separation of the actual and visual spatial quantums are both fundamental characteristics of the Baroque. And the architecture of the Baroque is indicated both by the tendency to unite by means of vertical lines and by the progression from the emphasis of the surface to the accentuation of the dominance of plastic elements. In this sense Palladio, undoubtedly the most important European architect between Michelangelo on the one hand and Bernini and Borromini on the other, can be described as decisive in preparing the way for the Baroque. However much Vignola may have contributed to the development of Baroque sacred architecture with the building of his church Il Gésu, which was begun in Rome in 1568, in the dissection of the wall surfaces into small parts both on the façade and inside, and with the clear fixing of the borders of the room, he remains far more deeply committed to the late Renaissance than Palladio's Il Redentore.

Individual works by Palladio have been emulated almost immeasurably both in the form of direct copies and of variations. Palladio's power to leave his mark both on the "style classique", that is the Baroque of France and England, and the Classicism of the late eighteenth and early nineteenth centuries, is unique.

But beyond this, we should recognise that Palladio, specifically with his later works, opened up the road to the entire field of European Baroque, which appeared in so many different forms.

"... you are romantic, Herbert always said to me, when I asked him to stop the car, because I wanted to look at one of these houses somewhere, he never took any notice of them, he always looked at churches and palazzi, at his Palladios and Sansovinos and Bramantis, the entire art historical rubbish ..."
(Alfred Andersch, The Red, 1960)

"The main point has been neglected most of all, and the crux of the fiction, the propriety of imitation, has rarely been understood when it was most needed, in transferring to private dwellings what was otherwise the sole property of temples and public buildings in order to give them a splendid appearance. One might maintain that in modern times a twofold fiction and multiple imitation have arisen in this way, and they require judgement and thought both in their use and in their assessment.
In this, none excelled Palladio. He moved with the greatest freedom on this road, and if he exceeded his bounds we always forgive him the faults we discover in him."
(Johann Wolfgang von Goethe, "Architecture", 1795)

Bibliography

Ackermann, James S., Palladio, London, 1966

Bertotti-Scamozzi, Le fabbriche e i disegni di Andrea Palladio, Vol. 1–4, Vicenza 1776–1783

Beyer, Andreas, Andrea Palladio. Das Teatro Olimpico, Frankfurt am Main, 1987

Constant, Caroline, Der Palladio Führer, Braunschweig, Wiesbaden, 1988

Forssmann, Erik, Palladios Lehrgebäude, Uppsala, 1965

Goethe, Johann Wolfgang von, Italian Journey, Penguin Classics

Lauritzen, Peter, Venice, London, 1978

Muraro, Michelangelo, Die Villen des Veneto, Munich, 1986

Murray, Peter, The Architecture of the Italian Renaissance, London, 1963

Muttoni, Francesco, Architettura di Andrea Palladio Vicentino con le osservazioni dell'Architetto N. N., 9 Vols, Venice, 1740–1748

Palladio, Andrea, The Venice edition of 1570, "I Quattro Libri dell'Architettura", translated from Italian into English by G. Leoni (London, 1715/20 and 1742, notes by Inigo Jones) and L. Ware (London, 1738)

Pée, Herbert, Die Palastbauten des Andrea Palladio, Würzburg, 1941

Puppi, Lionello, Andrea Palladio, London, 1975

Vitruvius, Des Marcus Vitruvius Pollio Baukunst, trans. August Rode, Zurich and Munich, 1982

Wittkower, R., Architectural Principles in the Age of Humanism, London, 1962

Zorzi, Alvise, Venedig – die Geschichte der Löwenrepublik, Düsseldorf, 1985

Maps giving positions of buildings

1. Villa Godi
2. Villa Piovene
3. Villa Forni-Cerato
4. Villa Gazotti
5. Villa Pisani (Bagnolo)
6. Villa Saraceno
7. Villa Thiene
8. Palazzo Thiene
9. Villa Poiana
10. Palazzo della Ragione (Basilica)
11. Palazzo Iseppo Porto
12. Palazzo Chiericati
13. Villa Cornaro
14. Villa Pisani (Montagnana)
15. Villa Chiericati
16. Palazzo Antonini
17. Villa Badoer
18. Villa Barbaro
19. Villa Foscari »La Malcontenta«
20. Santa Maria della Carità
21. San Giorgio Maggiore
22. Il Redentore
23. Villa Emo
24. Palazzo Valmarana
25. Palazzo Schio
26. La Rotonda
27. Villa Sarego
28. San Francesco della Vigna
29. Palazzo Barbarano
30. Loggia del Capitaniato
31. Palazzo Porto – Breganze
32. Le Zitelle
33. Teatro Olimpico
34. Tempietto Barbaro

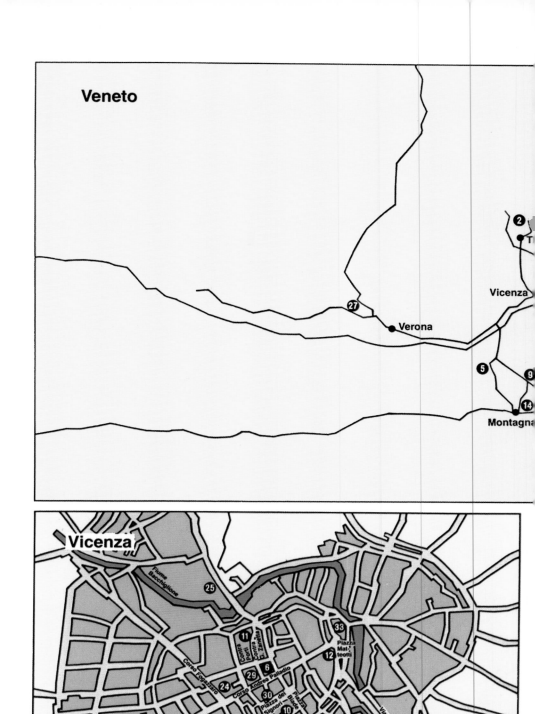

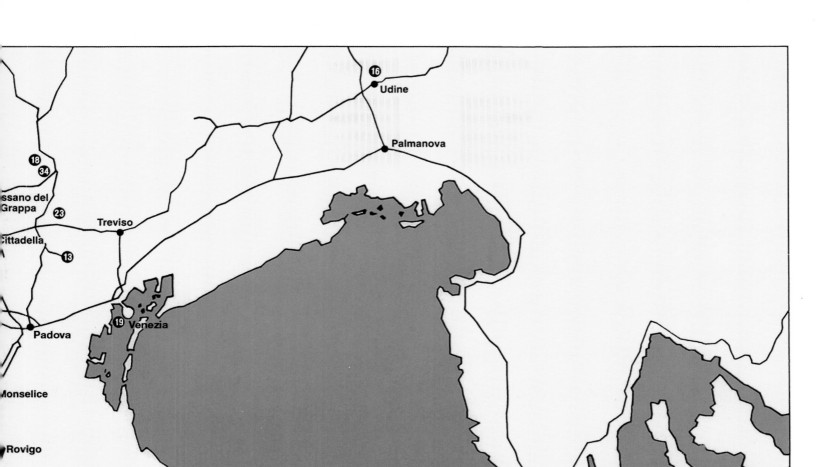

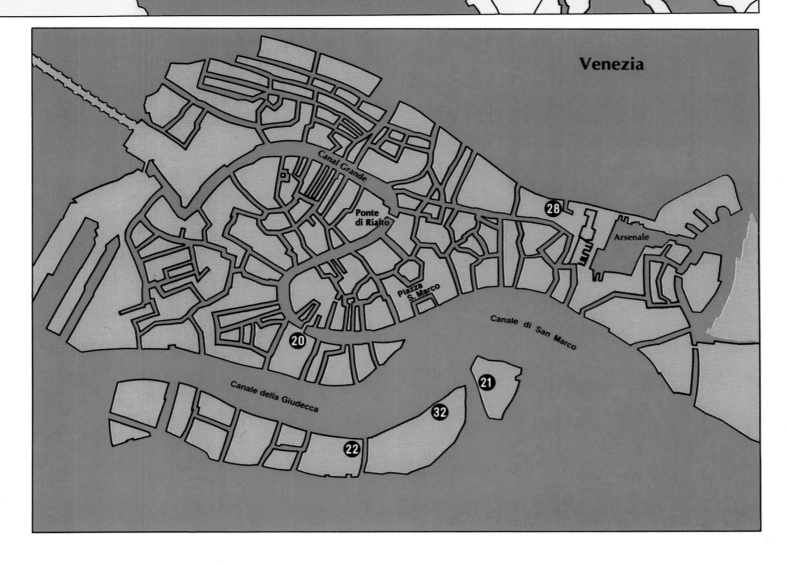

Venezia

Canal Grande

Ponte di Rialto

Piazza S. Marco

Arsenale

Canale di San Marco

Canale della Giudecca

Architectural Terms

Architrave
horizontal beam, part of an entablature, which carries the upper part of a building

Arcade
an arrangement of arches consisting of pillars that bear arches

Attic storey
low storey above the main entablature of a building. It usually has another ledge above it

Barchesses
arch arrangements or colonnades in front of a villa's agricultural wings

Bosses
rough stones unworked at the front; part of rustication

Bucranium
ox-skull used with triglyphs as part of the decorations of Doric entablatures. Several bucraniums are often used next to each other: such a frieze is called a Bucrane frieze

Columbaries
(columba, Latin: dove) dove-cotes

Consoles
stones that project from the surface of the façade

Crossing or crossways
space at the intersection of nave and transepts

Drum
vertical, often circular, wall supporting a dome

Etablature
upper part of an order, consisting of architrave, frieze and cornice

Feet (Vicenzan)
Palladio gives his buildings' measurements in Vicenzan feet, dividing each into twelve inches and those into four minutes. Feet varied from town to town, but normally meant a distance of 30 cm. The Venetian foot was about 35 cm.

Flutes
concave grooves on the shafts of columns

Iconography
involves the study of pictorial programmes, and of representative art in general

Intercolumnation
the space between two columns, measured from centre to centre of the columns

Lantern
small turret with windows that let in light, usually on a dome

Loggia
hall or open walkway on the front of a building

Metope
plastically decorated area (by means of bucraniums or round discs, for example) between the triglyph areas of the Doric order. In some buildings, Palladio shaped his Doric frieze by regularly alternating triglyph-disc-triglyph-bucranium

Mezzanine
half-storey which incorporated servants' and working rooms

Oculi
round windows

Peristyle courtyard
courtyard surrounded by a colonnade

Piano nobile
main storey of a building

Pilasters
rectangular column with pedestals and capitals

Proscenium
raised stage in front of the scenae frons

Risalito
part of a building that projects in front of, and is as high as, the rest of the building

Rustication
execution of a façade with roughly cut stone (bosses)

Sala
main room of the piano nobile

scenae frons
part of a theatre. It is the architectuarally structured back wall of the stage

Serliana
archway with three openings, the two side ones having straight tops with entablatures. Ancient motif, that was frequently used by Serlio, and was develped further by Palladio, and is also called the Palladio motif

Telamones
male figures that support an entablature

Terraferma
mainland possessions of the Republic of Venice

Triglyph
part of a Doric frieze, having three vertical grooves

Upper gallery
admits light to the centre aisle of a basilica. It is raised above the side aisles that border the centre aisle

248